THE POWER OF
IGNORANCE

Also by Dave Trott

Creative Mischief
Predatory Thinking
One Plus One Equals Three: A Masterclass in Creative Thinking
Creative Blindness

THE POWER OF IGNORANCE

HOW CREATIVE SOLUTIONS EMERGE WHEN WE ADMIT WHAT WE DON'T KNOW

Dave Trott

HARRIMAN HOUSE LTD
3 Viceroy Court
Bedford Road
Petersfield
Hampshire
GU32 3LJ
GREAT BRITAIN
Tel: +44 (0)1730 233870

Email: enquiries@harriman-house.com
Website: harriman.house

First published in 2021

Paperback ISBN: 978-0-85719-835-8
eBook ISBN: 978-0-85719-836-5

British Library Cataloguing in Publication Data
A CIP catalogue record for this book can be obtained from the British Library.

Cover design by Jade Trott.

CONTENTS

CONTENTS

ABOUT THE AUTHOR

Dave Trott is a creative director, copywriter and author. He studied at the Pratt Institute in New York City, majoring in advertising before going on to found the advertising agencies Gold Greenlees Trott, Bainsfair Sharkey Trott and Walsh Trott Chick Smith. In 2004 he was given the D&AD President's Award for lifetime achievement in advertising. He has also received lifetime achievement in advertising awards from The Creative Circle, The Marketing Society, and The Scottish Advertising Association.

Dave is married with two children and lives in London. *The Power of Ignorance* is his fifth book.

INTRODUCTION

I always learned more from stories than from lectures.

This book is written for people like me.

There's a story about an American student of Buddhism who travels to the mountains to see an elderly Buddhist master.

He wishes to learn from him, so they sit cross-legged on the floor as tea is served.

The student is nervous, he wants to impress the master with his knowledge.

He starts telling him everything he knows about Buddhism.

The master begins pouring tea into the student's cup.

The student mentions all the books he has read, every famous teacher he has studied.

The master continues pouring tea into the student's cup.

The student mentions every monastery he has visited, he begins to get nervous as his cup begins to fill.

The master continues to pour tea into the cup.

The student is talking faster and faster about all the different forms of meditation he has tried, he can't take his eyes off the cup which is now full to the brim.

The master continues pouring and the cup overflows.

The master continues pouring as the tea runs across the table and down onto the floor.

The student shouts: **"Stop, stop, why are you still pouring? The cup is full, it can't take anymore."**

The teacher says: **"Your mind is like this cup – it is so full there is no room for anything else. Like the cup, you must empty your mind before it can accept anything new."**

That is the problem most of us have.

We are scared stiff to let go of what we know, we acquire knowledge and cling onto it, consequently we can never learn anything new.

As Adlai Stevenson said: **"Most people approach every problem with an open mouth."**

We feel we must be the first to offer a solution.

We think knowledge is strength and ignorance is weakness.

But all that actually ensures is we offer a solution from the range of options that already exist, we never learn anything new.

We never learn anything new because we never ask questions.

We never ask questions because we're afraid to say **"I don't know."**

We never say **"I don't know"** so we can never discover anything new.

Our cup is full to overflowing.

Socrates was involved in a discussion with Meno, who believed his forceful opinion would win him the argument.

Socrates said: **"I am wiser than this man, for neither of us appears to know anything great and good, but he fancies he knows something, although he knows nothing; whereas I, as I do not know anything, so I do not fancy I do. In this trifling particular, then, I appear to be wiser than he, because I do not fancy I know what I do not know."**

Lao Tzu (the father of Taoism) put it more simply: **"The wise man knows he doesn't know. The fool doesn't know he doesn't know."**

What both of these men were saying concerns the way to approach a problem.

Contrary to the conventional belief, there is actually weakness in knowledge and strength in ignorance.

Ignorance, properly used with curiosity, allows us to find out things we didn't know.

And that NEW knowledge allows us to come up with new solutions.

Solutions that weren't visible from the previous position of existing knowledge.

This entire book is about asking questions, because creativity is about asking questions.

Using ignorance as a torch, to uncover what everyone else has walked over, unaware.

Because ignorance coupled with curiosity results in questions that no one else is asking.

Questions like: how could Pepsi sell cola to Russia when Coca-Cola couldn't?

How did IBM build the biggest computer company in the world in a depression?

How could a madman and a murderer be the saviour of the English language?

How do you sell glassware to people who've already got all the glassware they need?

How did George Washington's friends kill him with too much knowledge?

How did the competition build Uber by trying to kill it?

How did an expert create the useless rule of passwords that everyone still believes?

How and why did Disney create the myth of lemmings?

How and why did the cleverest and most famous people in the world lose billions?

How do you build a brand out of purposely not having any brand at all?

Our mind is like that student's cup.

We can't put anything new into it until we first empty it.

That's how we use ignorance, as a tool to empty the cup so we can fill it with new knowledge.

Ignorance coupled with curiosity is where all new knowledge starts.

Ignorance, used properly, is our secret weapon.

PART 1

WHAT YOU DON'T KNOW YOU DON'T KNOW

THE ANSWER ASKS THE QUESTION

In 1942, Britain was losing the battle of the Atlantic, which meant they were losing the war.

This has a way of concentrating the mind, so they were prepared to try anything.

One of the desperate moves was to try war-gaming.

All that could be spared was a retired naval officer and eight young Wrens, for a group called Western Approaches Tactical Unit (WATU).

The young Wrens knew nothing of anti-submarine warfare of course.

This meant they had lots of questions.

As with any problem, questions are always a good place to start.

Q) Whereabouts in the convoy are the ships being attacked?

A) Usually in the centre, at night.

Q) How big is the convoy?

A) About 8 miles square.

Q) What is the torpedoes' range?

A) About 2 miles.

Conclusion: the U-boats must be attacking from inside the convoy. Torpedoes can't reach the centre from outside.

Q) What is the convoy's speed?

A) Around 10 knots.

Q) What is a U-boat's speed?

A) 16 knots on the surface, 6 knots submerged.

Conclusion: the U-boats are attacking on the surface, they are too slow when submerged.

Q) How long does it take to reload the torpedoes?

A) About half an hour.

Q) Would they do this on the surface?

A) No, they would submerge.

<u>Conclusion</u>: after an attack, a U-boat will submerge and be left behind by the convoy.

They will then have to surface to catch up.

In having to answer the Wrens' questions, the naval officer had to think like a U-boat commander, and that was the first time anyone had done that.

Instead of rushing around after the first ship exploded, they realised the destroyers had some time while the U-boat reloaded.

They could let the convoy pass on and, after it was gone, search for the U-boats that were reloading.

Because they were submerged they were slower, and the destroyers could use ASDIC (underwater radar) to locate them.

But first they had to prove it to the Admiral in charge, so they used a war game.

Admiral Sir Max Horton was an ex-submariner.

He took the role of a U-boat captain.

Five times he attacked the convoy, five times he was sunk by his unseen opponent, using these new tactics.

He asked to be introduced to his opponent, who he hadn't even seen yet.

His opponent was 18-year-old Wren, Janet Okell, who'd been helping devise the new tactics.

The Admiral was convinced, and the tactics began sinking U-boats for real in the Atlantic.

WATU was expanded to eight male officers and 36 Wren officers and ratings.

During the war, they trained 5,000 naval officers in anti-submarine warfare.

At the end of the battle of the Atlantic, 75% of all U-boats had been destroyed.

They discovered the value of asking new questions is you come up with new answers.

Which wouldn't have happened without having to train those Wrens.

Asking questions that hadn't been asked before wasn't silly, in fact it won the battle of the Atlantic.

THE POWER OF NICHE

At Gwyneth Paltrow's site, goop, you could buy a candle labelled: SMELLS LIKE MY VAGINA for just seventy-five dollars.

Naturally, the online media went wild with outrage and jokes.

It was only on sale for a few days and it sold out straightaway.

Never mind, if you're too late to get one, you can still buy one of her Vaginal Eggs.

They're made from jade and cost just sixty dollars apiece.

Again, when they first went on sale, she was completely ridiculed in the press and on TV.

But if vaginal jade eggs aren't your thing, there's always her Vaginal Steaming.

You sit over mugwort-infused steam and feel the benefit.

Again, the media was beside itself with disdain and disbelief.

Paltrow was interviewed about it, in magazines and on TV chat shows all over the world.

The interesting thing is that goop hardly advertise, and yet it's one of the most famous, most talked about brands in the world.

There are 2.4 million visitors to the site every month, and up to 600,000 listeners a week to the podcasts, and a Netflix series.

Every time she needs some publicity, Paltrow simply releases another story about a vaginal product and the media goes crazy.

She gets free coverage that would cost hundreds of millions of dollars.

The New York Times said: "The weirder goop went the more its readers rejoiced. Every time there was a negative story about her or her company all it did was bring more people to the site."

Paltrow told a class of Harvard students: "What I do is create a cultural firestorm, and I can monetize those eyeballs."

The focus of so much ridicule, goop is now valued at a quarter of a billion dollars.

The lesson is, Paltrow is targeting the opposite of mass media. She wants women who see themselves as confident, individual, and discerning: women with money.

When the mass media is outraged, she has simply provoked another advertising campaign.

Obviously, goop doesn't make money from its vaginal products.

But what it does get is an enormous amount of publicity.

The vaginal products are the advertising equivalent of loss-leaders in retail: products which get people into the store in order to buy other things.

Like: earrings for $3,900, or trousers for $790, or a jump suit for $1,395, or boots for $860, or T-shirts for $145, or bracelets for $4,775, or shoes for $650.

Those items make money, but none of those things would attract any publicity.

She tried selling Psychic Vampire Repellent for $27, a Medicine Bag of Gemstones for $85, even a 24-carat gold-plated vibrator for $15,000, but none of these things attracted as much free publicity as the vagina products.

Because none of them caused the outrage that goop needed as fuel for controversy.

And that really is the lesson here.

There's an enormous amount of money to be made in what we perceive as niche.

I remember when Saatchi was one of the biggest ad agencies in the UK, apparently it had just 2% of the market, in other words for every person that wanted it, 49 didn't.

Which leads us to the power of polarisation.

Once you know the niche your market's in, you can spend a lot of time publicly turning off everyone else.

Like Saatchi, you don't need 100% of people to find you bland and okay.

You need 2% of people to love you, even if that means 98% of people hate you.

By focussing on her niche, Paltrow built a $250 million business, almost without advertising.

By shocking the people her market didn't want to be like.

IT'S NOT WHERE YOU START IT'S WHERE YOU FINISH

The chainsaw was invented for chopping down trees, right?

Wrong, the chainsaw was invented for helping women give birth.

But how can that be true?

Well, until two hundred years ago, childbirth wasn't pleasant for the mother.

Especially if, for whatever reason, the baby wouldn't fit through her opening.

The main medical tools of the time were knives, saws, chisels, and mallets.

If the baby was too large, or turned the wrong way, the opening had to be widened.

This involved cutting away bone and cartilage, and lots of pain (because there were no anaesthetics).

The process was called a symphysiotomy: the pelvis had to be cut and expanded, in order to make the opening wider.

This was such an unpleasant procedure that two Scottish doctors independently invented a tool to make it more efficient.

They invented the chainsaw.

The chainsaw was a tool with a chain of saw-teeth that was hand-cranked.

In 1783, John Aitken illustrated his device in *Principles of Midwifery, Or Puerperal Medicine.*

In 1790, James Jeffray developed his own version and wrote about it in *Cases of the Excision of Carious Joints.*

Their chainsaws were an improvement on the surgeon's saw, which had to be inserted into the opening and pulled and pushed back and forth, while the legs were held apart.

At least with the chainsaw the surgeon just held it in place and turned the crank.

Obviously the principle of continuous motion over reciprocating motion was better for the patient, but it was also a more efficient use of energy.

In 1905, Samuel J. Bens spotted this and used it for the giant redwoods he was logging.

When men sawed back and forth, every stroke had to stop, and reverse, and waste energy.

But with a chainsaw the movement was in one direction only, there was no wasted energy.

And he was granted US Patent 780,476 for his 'endless chain saw'.

Enlarging surgical chainsaws up to tree-felling size meant they were huge and cumbersome, but still had to be cranked by hand.

So in 1926, Andreas Stihl invented the electric-powered chainsaw, and in 1929 the petrol-powered version.

In the 1950s the chainsaw became smaller and portable, to the point where one person could operate one on their own.

And today, most people wouldn't believe you if you told them where chainsaws started off.

But that's the way it is with ideas.

An idea doesn't pop out fully formed and stop there forever.

An idea gets changed, improved, and repurposed.

That's the difference between pure math and applied math, between pure art and applied art.

One person makes a discovery, another person decides what it can be used for.

We don't usually invent something from scratch, we repurpose an idea that already exists.

Something the original innovator didn't even see when they created it.

That's how creativity works, in incremental stages, each stage is a new creative vision.

As film maker Jean-Luc Godard said: **"It's not where you take something from, it's where you take it to."**

Or as the best advertising art director ever, Helmut Krone, said: **"First you make the revolution, then you decide what it's for."**

HOW TO WIN BY GIVING IN

When Steve Jobs returned to Apple, the smartest things he did was spot Jonathan Ive.

Ive was about to quit, Jobs persuaded him to stay.

Subsequently, Ive designed products like: the iMac, the iPod, the iPhone, the iPad.

Each design was groundbreaking, other firms could only do poor copies.

But Ive freely admits, his inspiration was another designer: Dieter Rams.

When you compare Ive's designs with Rams' you can clearly see the influence.

Dieter Rams began life as a designer in 1955 when he joined Braun.

For the next forty years he revolutionised domestic appliance design: from radios to kitchen mixers, from record players to electric razors, from watches to TV sets.

Today there are museums full of his work in cities from London to New York to Tokyo.

But for me, the most creative thing that happened wasn't anything he did.

It was a decision taken by the two brothers who employed him, Artur and Erwin Braun.

Rams had been working for Braun for about five years when he was approached by a designer friend, Otto Zapf.

Zapf was opening a furniture design company with Niels Vitsoe.

They wanted to know if Rams could help them out by doing a bit of freelance design.

Rams hadn't done furniture before, but he was happy to try.

He designed the furniture the same way he designed the Braun products: minimalist, functional, practical.

His designs were successful, so they asked him to do more and more.

Rams decided this was becoming a conflict of interest.

The Braun brothers were paying him to be their designer, but he was also working for someone else.

So he went to see Artur and Erwin Braun and asked them if should stop freelancing.

And here's the really creative part for me.

Most companies would immediately say: **"Of course you must quit your freelance, we're paying you to design for us not someone else."**

But the brothers didn't say that.

They said: **"Go ahead, we don't make furniture so there is no conflict. In fact, if people buy your furniture it can only be good for Braun."**

That decision, for me, is the really creative leap.

What they'd realised was that, in the 1950s, most homes were furnished with old-fashioned heavy, upholstered wood and cloth furniture.

People wouldn't buy Braun's minimalist, metal and plastic, functional designs to go with furniture like that.

But if younger people began to furnish their apartments with modern minimalist furniture, made from plastic and metal, then Braun products would fit perfectly.

So, by letting Rams design furniture they were creating their own market.

And that's exactly what happened.

Rams designed bookshelves, and chairs, and tables, and sofas and all of his furniture designs fitted perfectly with all his home appliance designs.

Both companies grew and, over the next few decades, changed the design aesthetic.

What we now recognise as good design came from Rams' furniture and Braun electronics.

Without them there would be no Habitat, no Ikea and, as Jonathan Ive admits, Apple certainly wouldn't look the way it does.

And it all happened because of the Braun brothers' creative decision to go against conventional wisdom and allow their top designer to freelance for someone else.

Which goes to show, sometimes the most creative thinkers aren't the 'creatives'.

SOMETHING FROM NOTHING

As we know, there are three kinds of media: paid-for media, owned media, and earned media.

The first two are easy. Paid-for media is any space you pay for: TV, print, OOH (out-of-home), online.

Owned media is anything you own that can be used as media: delivery trucks, shop windows, packaging, mail.

But the real creative opportunity is the third one: earned media.

This is where no media exists until you make it happen.

An example would be the El Paso Zoo in Texas.

To attract visitors, they needed to get people talking about the zoo to make it more relevant, more topical and interesting.

What could they do that was different, that would get people talking, what would earn free media?

Valentine's Day was coming up, every zoo would be doing the usual – adopt a pair of lovebirds, or similar.

How about if they went in the exact opposite direction?

Instead of celebrating the few happy couples, what if they went for a larger market?

Everyone's had their heart broken, and a lot of people think Valentine's Day is just another cynical way to make money.

Nobody is talking to that market, so the zoo could have that all to themselves.

And that's exactly what they did.

On their Facebook page, they advertised that they would be happy to name a cockroach after your ex and feed it to a meerkat live online, on Valentine's Day.

The event was called QUIT BUGGING ME.

You simply left a message on Facebook with your ex's first name and initial, then at 2.15 on Valentine's Day the cockroaches would be fed to the meerkats.

Meerkats love them, large Madagascar hissing cockroaches are specially bred to supplement their diet.

Just days after that post on Facebook, 1,500 people had already left messages with the name of their ex.

Some, from as far away as Germany and Australia, were even organising parties to watch their ex get eaten.

The promotion was covered by TV, newspapers, and online media around the world, all for free.

That's earned media – it didn't exist until they had the idea, and it didn't cost a penny.

A few years before, Woodland Park Zoo in Seattle had a different idea.

It wasn't earned media, but it also created something from nothing.

They noticed they were paying $90,000 a year to get all their animal dung removed.

They thought, how about if we turn that round: if we don't pay someone to take it away but we sell it.

And they began selling ZOO POO fertilizer at $20 for a two-gallon drum.

It's a much better fertilizer because it only comes from herbivores: giraffes, hippos, gazelles, and zebras and it's mixed with straw, grass, leaves, and woodchips.

Garden plants don't have to rely on artificially mass-produced fertilizer made in factories.

Plus, they also sell WORM POO for $10 a pint.

This is compost that worms have eaten and expelled, so it has the added benefit of being **'twice pooped'**, and therefore exceptionally rich in nutrients for seedlings and potted plants

These zoos made something from nothing: no money, no media, no strategists, no brief.

And yet they're more creative than most of us.

DON'T OUTPLAY THEM, OUT-THINK THEM

Liverpool's fourth goal against Barcelona in the 2019 Champions League semi-final.

The ball went out for a corner, Trent Alexander-Arnold carefully placed it then walked away.

Then he turned, ran back and crossed it.

And, while Barcelona were standing still, Divock Origi ran in and scored for Liverpool.

Liverpool came back from 3-0 down in the first game, to win the second game 4-0.

They knocked out the best team in the world and were going to the Champions League final.

That's why everyone loves that cheeky goal.

But it wasn't just the result of an instinctively taken half-chance.

It was the result of careful preparation.

Before that match, Liverpool had their analysts look for weaknesses in Barcelona.

It's very tough to find weaknesses in the best team in the world.

But one thing they did notice was they argued about every decision that went against them.

These were the best players in the world and their egos told them they were right, so the referee must be wrong.

Besides which, if a referee doesn't quite see the foul, you can often get him to give the decision your way.

So, it seemed to be worth arguing over every decision.

The Liverpool analysts had noticed it and told Jürgen Klopp it could be a weakness: while they were arguing they weren't concentrating.

So Klopp talked to Carl Lancaster, the head of the coaching academy.

The boys at the academy are also the ballboys for Liverpool's games.

Lancaster showed them videos of Barcelona arguing after the ball had gone out of play.

He made the ballboys realise that if they could get the ball back really fast, Barcelona wouldn't be ready for it.

So the ballboys worked on that all week.

It seems a tiny thing, but delivering the ball fast was what lead to Liverpool's fourth goal.

The ballboy was 14-year-old Oakley Cannonier.

He was prepared so, when the ball went out for a corner, he didn't even have to run and get it, he had a spare ball ready.

He instantly rolled it to Alexander-Arnold while Barcelona were arguing.

Alexander-Arnold placed it and walked away, as if leaving it for someone else.

He casually looked up to see where Origi was, then turned and kicked the ball over the heads of all the still arguing Barcelona players.

Because they were arguing, their defence was completely out of position.

Before they finished arguing, the ball was in their net, Liverpool were 4-0 up, and Barcelona were out of the Champions League.

All because of attention to detail and thorough planning.

All down to looking for an opportunity where no one else was looking.

Spotting something no one else had spotted.

That's what competition is, that's what creativity is at its best.

As Schopenhauer said: **"Talent hits a target no one else can hit. Genius hits a target no one else can see."**

That's what creative thinking is, creating an unfair advantage.

Bill Bernbach spotted it before anyone else, that's why he said:

"It may well be that creativity is the last unfair advantage we're legally allowed to take over the competition."

In other words, if you can't outplay them, out-think them.

ADVERTISING AS CAMOUFLAGE

In 2008, Anthony Curcio needed twenty-five men to help him on a job in Monroe, Washington.

So he advertised on Craigslist, the pay was good, $28.50 an hour.

Landscaping work, but you had to come dressed ready to start: jeans, blue shirt, work shoes, yellow safety vest, safety goggles, and a painter's mask.

The meeting place was in the Bank of America parking lot, September 9th.

At the time stated in the ad, dozens of men showed up dressed and ready.

They looked around for the boss, but there were just lots of other men dressed like them.

Then a Brink's armoured car pulled in outside the Bank of America, and the guard went into the bank.

A minute or so later the guard came out with two sacks of money.

Suddenly one of the landscapers pepper-sprayed the guard, grabbed the sacks, and ran off.

Everyone stood around wondering what the hell was happening, it must be a robbery.

Eventually the police showed up and asked for a description of the robber.

All anyone could repeat was what he was wearing: jeans, blue shirt, work shoes, yellow safety vest, safety goggles, and a painter's mask.

Just like the dozens of other men standing around in the car park.

The police checked all the VCR cameras, but everyone fitted exactly that description.

Because the job Anthony Curcio advertised on Craigslist wasn't what everyone thought.

It wasn't a landscaping job, it was a bank job and he escaped with $400,000.

He did it by reversing conventional wisdom.

He didn't make himself blend into the environment, he changed the environment to blend in with him.

He had been setting up the robbery for weeks, dressed as someone nobody would notice, a landscaper: sweeping up, picking weeds, cutting grass.

He noted the days and times the armoured car came, when it had the biggest bags of cash.

He noted the number of guards, their security routine.

All he needed on the day of the robbery was to make sure no one could identify him.

So he advertised for several dozen people dressed exactly like him to be standing around in that spot at exactly that time.

It was a new take on camouflage.

Fitting in so no one will notice you, because that's what he wanted, not to be noticed.

But that's pretty much the opposite of what we want.

If we fit in and no one notices us we've wasted our money.

If no one notices us we may as well not be running any advertising at all.

If we look like all the other ads around us, we'll be as invisible and we'll escape unnoticed.

But is that really what we want our advertising to do, escape unnoticed?

Every time I do a talk I make the point that, if you live in a major conurbation, you're exposed to around 2,000 advertising messages a day.

Press ads, OOH, radio ads, pre-rolls on YouTube, ads on Facebook and Twitter, 16 and 48 sheet crosstracks on the Tube, commercials on Freeview or Sky, plus all the rest, that's 2,000 advertising messages a day.

Then I ask: **"As a consumer, hold your hand up if you remember one from yesterday."**

Out of an audience of 200, usually six, maybe ten hands go up.

So, do the math, 200 times 2,000 ads each, equals 400,000 ads.

So 400,000 ad exposures and, every time I do it, around ten ads are even remembered twenty-four hours later.

I think we're doing a pretty good job of camouflaging ourselves.

WE REALLY WANT WHAT WE CAN'T HAVE

In 1503, a Florentine artist took on a commission for a local businessman, Francesco del Giocondo.

It was a painting of his wife, it wasn't considered anything special.

It wasn't big, it measured 30" × 21" (between modern sizes A1 and A2).

But around 300 years later, in 1797, it ended up on the wall between much larger pictures in the Louvre in Paris.

The public barely noticed it, until 21st August 1911.

On that day, Vincenzo Peruggia visited the Louvre and hid in a broom closet.

After the museum closed he came out and took the small painting off the wall, it fitted under his coat so he took it and calmly walked out of the building.

No one even noticed anything unusual until sometime the next day.

Then someone remembered that there used to be a small picture in the gap between those two larger pictures.

No big deal, it must have been removed for cleaning.

Eventually they found it hadn't, and they realised this was an art theft.

But not just any theft, the thief ignored all the other masterpieces and targeted this painting.

It must be worth more than anything else hanging on the walls.

The newspapers got hold of the story and everyone wanted to know what this masterpiece was that had been targeted above all the others.

The Louvre checked and told them it was known as the **Mona Lisa**.

The public didn't remember it, but it was obviously the most valuable painting in the Louvre.

Suddenly everyone wanted to see the **Mona Lisa**.

They must see the painting that was worth stealing above all others.

But no one could see it, because it wasn't there, which made them want to see it more.

The **Mona Lisa** soon became the most famous painting in the world.

It was as if the Louvre was only half the museum without it.

Eventually, after two years, it was recovered when the thief tried to sell it to the Uffizi gallery in Florence.

It was quickly returned to the Louvre and everyone packed in to see it.

Today, according to director Henri Loyrette, six million people visit the Louvre every year just to see the **Mona Lisa**.

This is known as the scarcity heuristic: people never want something so much as when they can't have it.

I saw the same thing at the National Gallery's Caravaggio exhibition.

The star exhibit was the painting **Supper at Emmaus**, the crowd was seven deep, people had to wait ages to glimpse it for a few seconds.

Yet for the rest of the year it was on permanent display upstairs in the main gallery.

You could look at it all day on your own if you wanted, but no one even bothered.

The producer, Mike Todd, knew all about the scarcity heuristic.

He had a play running in Manhattan that wasn't at all successful.

So he hired a lady with arthritic fingers for the box office.

When someone wanted a ticket it took her ages to give them their change.

The people behind them had to wait and this caused a queue.

Seeing the queue, other people joined, figuring it must be a good show.

The queue got longer and people passing decided they couldn't miss out, so they joined.

Eventually, the queue was round the block.

Mike Todd's show became a huge success, thanks to the lady with arthritic fingers who unwittingly utilised the scarcity heuristic.

EVERYONE NEEDS A SECOND CHANCE

California has more cars and drivers than any state in the USA.

So naturally, they also have more car crashes, and consequently more fatalities.

95% of people in California think organ donation is a good thing.

Every organ donor has the potential to save eight lives, and enhance up to 75 others, via organs, eyes, and tissue donation.

But only 45% of drivers have actually signed up as organ donors.

That means 114,000 people are waiting for organs.

Why the discrepancy?

To become an organ donor you need to fill out forms and get a pink dot stamped on your licence.

But to renew your licence you have to go to the Department of Motor Vehicles (DMV).

This is a famously unpleasant experience: the queues are long, everyone is grumpy, they can't wait to get out of there.

So ad agency Casanova//McCann and the client, Donate Life CA, took a new look at the problem.

Instead of nagging non-users with posters, in the DMV queue, how about rewarding current users?

People who already had the pink dot on their licence.

So everyone would see the whole experience was a lot more pleasant.

And they created an idea called SECOND CHANCE.

They had a logo made out of two number 2s facing each other, like a heart.

They persuaded three police departments in California, Fullerton, Placentia, and Cal State, plus Calgary in Canada, to get involved.

The idea was that when a driver was about to get a traffic ticket for a minor violation, if the officer saw a pink dot on their driving licence, indicating they were a donor, he could give them a second chance.

And they made a film recording how the idea worked in action.

The film showed officers stopping drivers for speeding or going through stop signs.

The officer would see their licence and fill out a ticket, as usual: Name, Address, City, State, Zip Code, Driver Licence Number, Description of Violation, Citing Officer.

But when he handed the ticket over to the driver, it was different.

It read:

"Instead of a fine, today you get a SECOND CHANCE.

Why?

1. **Because you're willing to give your fellow citizens a second chance at life, by registering as an organ donor.**

2. **Because only half of Americans are registered donors, and you're changing that statistic.**

3. **Because the police department wants to thank you for doing something for others.**

4. **Because we want to remind you how easy it is to be a hero."**

The film shows the immense relief on the faces of the drivers when they receive it.

The officer thanks them and says how much everyone appreciates their donation.

110,000 drivers signed up as donors in one month (that's 30,773 more than the same month in the previous year).

Those extra donors have the potential to save 246,184 lives.

But the really creative part is they didn't nag non-donors with facts and figures.

They showed them what they were missing out on.

Now organ donations are up, people are alive who wouldn't be.

And the police enjoy the more positive interaction with the community.

Real creativity works for everyone.

READING THE SIGNS

At art school, in New York, I had a class called Visual Communication.

Today, this is known as semiotics: language without words.

At the time, it was a difficult class.

Words were the only communication I knew about, but actually that wasn't true.

Words were the only communication I was conscious of, but there was so much non-verbal communication I wasn't aware of.

Consequently, we learnt about packaging, typography, colour, shapes, sounds, movement, editing, even body language.

Another expression for semiotics is the study of signs.

And the purest, most powerful form of that was road signs.

Information that had to be stripped down to its simplest, most impactful.

Signs that could mean the difference between life and death.

In Britain, we have one of the best systems of road sign language in the world.

It was designed by Margaret Calvert in the 1960s.

She had recently graduated from Chelsea School of Art and, together with Jock Kinneir, she was given the brief for signage on the UK's first motorway.

There was to be no speed limit, and no one knew how anyone would be able to read a stationary sign when someone was travelling at 100 mph.

So clarity was everything.

Which is why I love the way Margaret Calvert researched her designs.

She took them to Benson Airfield in Oxfordshire and fixed them to the top of a car.

Then, at different speeds, she drove them towards a group of seated airmen.

And then she found out at what distance and what speed they could read the signs.

That's something most designers won't do, they'll judge their designs in an office on a table.

But her designs couldn't work like that.

Her designs weren't about subjective preferences, like whether anyone liked them.

Her designs had to communicate, it was semiotics in its purest form.

So they were judged in the context they had to work in, moving at speeds up to 100 mph.

Which is why they are such superb examples of clarity.

The motorway signs were such a success that she was asked to design the signage for the entire road system.

This isn't an exercise in style, this is an exercise in making the complicated simple.

The different roads had different speed limits and needed different information.

So she broke it down as follows:

Motorways would be white on blue.

A roads would be white on green (with numbers in yellow).

B roads would be black on white.

And there would be a simple system to emphasise what was being communicated.

So shapes were introduced as follows:

Triangles for warnings.

Circles for commands.

Squares for information.

As Margaret Calvert said: **"Direction signs are as vital as a drop of oil in an engine, without which the moving parts would seize up."**

No decoration, no subjectivity, no emotional preferences.

Just the functional clarity needed for the job.

Nothing to do with whether anyone involved liked it or not.

Pure semiotics: purely about how well it worked.

I wish more people could learn to think like that.

PART 2

WE CAN'T KNOW WHAT HASN'T HAPPENED

WHEN EXPERTS ARE THE PROBLEM

The atomic age began in 1945.

America was the only country with access to nuclear technology.

Even though Britain had helped them develop it, the US government wouldn't share any information.

The UK would just have to go it alone, so they did.

In 1952, they began planning a massive nuclear establishment at Windscale in Cumbria, thirty miles from Scotland.

The pressure was on to build it fast.

As it was nearing completion, one of the physicists, Terence Price, questioned whether they should have backup safety equipment, like filters.

All the other experts involved on the project ignored the suggestion.

Things were moving fast and they were already mid-construction.

But Sir John Cockcroft was Director of the Atomic Energy Research Establishment and in charge of the project, and the question of filters stayed with him.

Then he heard that particles of uranium oxide had been found in the vicinity of the American X-10 graphite reactor at Oak Ridge, Tennessee.

That convinced him, the chimneys on the nuclear reactors at Windscale must have filters to trap any escaping particles.

But the experts said it was expensive, time-consuming, and unnecessary.

The reactors were perfectly safe, no particles would escape, and anyway the 360-foot-tall chimneys were already built.

The place to have put the filters would have been at the bottom, before they were built.

But Cockcroft insisted, if they couldn't be added at the bottom they'd be added at the top.

Even though Leonard Owen, the Assistant Controller of the Department of Atomic Energy Production, had said they'd have two tons of boiling hot air going up those chimneys every second at 20 mph.

All the experts said it was a waste of time and money because the reactor was perfectly safe and the filters would never get used.

But Cockcroft insisted and two massive filters were added to the tops of the 360-foot-tall chimneys.

They looked ridiculous, they could be seen for miles around and they became known as "Cockcroft's Follies".

They were called that right up until October 10th, 1957.

That night they discovered radioactive fuel in the reactor was on fire and had been burning at 1,300 centigrade for two days.

It burned for another three days before it could be put out, releasing the deadly iodine-131.

It held the record for thirty years as Europe's worst nuclear disaster, up until Chernobyl.

But the filters on top of the chimneys ("Cockcroft's Follies" the things the experts said would never be used) caught 95% of the radioactive particles that were released.

A 1987 survey showed that there were no deaths at Windscale, though a potential (but highly unlikely) 33 future deaths.

At Chernobyl, by comparison, there were 47 deaths and a potential 9,000 future deaths.

Thanks to "Cockcroft's Follies" (which the experts said were a waste of time and money) 1,000 times fewer particles were released at Windscale than at Chernobyl.

Sir John Cockcroft stuck by his principle and suffered ridicule for it.

But without his stubbornness, many more people would have been dead and a large part of northern England still uninhabitable.

Sir John Cockcroft didn't listen to the experts, he listened to common sense.

Proving that sometimes we really do know better than the experts.

HAPPY ACCIDENTS

We assume everything is always the result of logical, straight-line thinking.

But that isn't always true.

For instance, take the rear-view mirror in your car.

The rear-view mirror was invented over 100 years ago by racing car driver Ray Harroun.

He was more of an engineer than a driver.

But he wanted to enter the first ever Indy 500 race in 1911, so he designed a racing car called the Marmon Wasp.

His first innovation was that his car was a single-seater.

In those days, every car had two seats, one for the driver, one for the mechanic.

The mechanic was there to fix the car if it broke down, and he would also tell the driver where the other cars were.

Ray Harroun knew his car wasn't going to break down so he didn't need a mechanic.

But on the day of the race, the other drivers complained.

Without a mechanic he would have no one to tell him where the other cars were, it could be a real danger to the other drivers.

That's when Ray Harroun showed them his second innovation.

He didn't need a mechanic to tell him because he made a large mirror with four metal legs, and he fitted it above the steering wheel.

That way, without taking his eyes off the road, he'd always know who was behind him.

No one had heard such an idea before, but they couldn't argue, it made sense.

So Ray Harroun started the race at number 28 out of 40.

Over the 6 hours and 42 minutes of the race he averaged 74.5 miles per hour.

A fast speed for 1911, but not as fast as some of the other drivers.

They would roar past, but they wore their tyres out and had to change them.

In 1911, tyre changing wasn't the speedy process it is in modern Formula One.

It was slow and cumbersome, which is where his opponents all lost time.

Ray Harroun only had to have four tyre changes.

His nearest opponent, Ralph Mumford, had to have fourteen tyre changes.

Ray Harroun won the first Indy 500 by over half a mile.

And he did it alone, without a mechanic looking around to help him.

The papers called his new device **'seeing without turning'** (the name rear-view mirror hadn't been invented yet).

Soon everybody wanted one, and today no car is made without one.

But it was only much later the truth came out.

After he retired, Ray Harroun explained the Indianapolis Speedway had been paved in 1910.

They'd used 3.2 million bricks and it was bumpy as hell.

As Ray said: **"It shook so bad I couldn't see a damn thing in the mirror anyway. But I made sure no one knew that but me."**

Ray kept it quiet because he didn't want to be disqualified.

The real purpose of the mirror wasn't to see what was happening behind anyway.

The real purpose was to let him race without a mechanic.

That meant his car was lighter than the others, and the tyres wouldn't wear out so fast.

That's all the mirror ever was, an excuse to get rid of the extra weight of a mechanic.

So the thing we all take for granted as a safety feature was never invented for that.

It was invented to get round the rules.

And today, every racing car is a single-seater, and every road car has a rear-view mirror.

Because creativity doesn't always work in straight lines.

It's good to remember that, because briefs aren't supposed to be straitjackets.

A brief should be the floor not the ceiling.

As John Webster always used to say to me: **"You have to leave room for accidents."**

CREATIVITY IS AMORAL

Wouldn't it make life easier if all the good people were creative and all the bad people weren't?

Unfortunately, it doesn't work like that.

Creativity lives in the realm of ideas, and bad people have ideas just like good people.

So we can either learn from everyone, or only learn from people we agree with.

Personally, I choose to learn from everyone.

Take Basil Zaharoff, born in 1849. He was senior partner in the Nordenfelt arms company.

He was responsible for sales of the Nordenfelt type 1 submarine.

It was driven by steam, which is not a great idea for a ship that submerges.

Zaharoff had already failed to sell a single submarine to any of the great naval powers: Britain, France, Germany, America.

They had large navies and saw no need to take a risk on a mere novelty.

The US criticised its **"dangerous and erratic movements"**, they found it **"chronically unstable"** and **"completely unacceptable"**.

So Zaharoff got creative.

If the countries with large navies didn't need it, what about the countries with no navies?

Zaharoff knew he needed a single sale to start the ball rolling.

So he explained to Greece how an underwater ship could be worth many surface ships.

It could approach unseen and, with its torpedoes, sink the battleships of larger nations.

And, because he was a loyal Greek, he would let them have it at half price.

The Greeks couldn't resist, they ordered a Nordenfelt type 1 submarine.

Having sold one submarine, Zaharoff then went to the Ottoman Empire.

He explained to the Turks how the Greeks could control the seas with their submarine.

Turkish ships would be helpless, but as a loyal Turkish subject he was willing to help them restore the balance of power.

The Turks were so grateful they ordered two Nordenfelt type 1 submarines.

Then Zaharoff went to see the Russians.

He explained that the Turks would soon have control of the Black Sea.

Because they now had two submarines capable of sinking any Russian ship that dared venture onto it.

As a loyal Russian subject it was his duty to help Mother Russia all he could.

The Russians were grateful for the tip and ordered two Nordenfelt type 1 submarines.

So Zaharoff sold five useless submarines because he understood two important things.

1. People who felt secure had no need to take chances, but people who felt insecure had to take chances.

2. People will judge what they need based on what their competition has.

Basil Zaharoff was not a nice man, but even bad men can be creative.

If we don't learn from everyone else, good and bad, we are like a horse with blinkers

Take Chernobyl, when Soviet scientists refused to listen to problems with the design of the nuclear power plant.

It had been designed by the Soviet state, and the Soviet state could not be wrong.

Western designs were said to be superior, but the West was capitalist and therefore evil, so everything the West did must be inferior.

Unfortunately, safe nuclear reactor design is neither capitalist nor communist.

By the time the Soviets accepted the faults in their design, 4,000 people were predicted to die.

All because they placed ideology before thinking.

That's the sort of thing we do when we believe only award-winning ads are good.

Only if a panel of judges, and the advertising press, has approved the ads.

And only if they're for products we approve of, with a brand purpose we like.

In a world where all the good guys are smart and all the bad guys are stupid.

A TOUCH OF GENIUS

Around 1800, Charles Barbier was an artillery officer in Napoleon's army.

One of the problems he noticed was the soldiers kept getting shot at night.

This was largely because, in order to read messages, they'd use a lamp.

Naturally, enemy snipers would use this as a target.

So Barbier decided they needed a safer way to communicate without light.

What if they could feel the message instead of seeing it?

And so he began to develop écriture nocturne – night writing.

He used a pattern of 12 dots in a rectangular shape, for each letter.

It worked but it was slow and complicated for soldiers to remember.

The army rejected it.

Then a 12-year-old student heard about it.

He'd been blinded playing with an awl in his father's workshop when he was a child.

In 1821 he met Charles Barbier and studied his system of night writing.

The student agreed with the army, it was too complicated.

But it didn't need to be, the basic idea was good, so he simplified it.

He changed the 12 dots for each letter to just 6, and instead of replicating the letters of the alphabet, it took the form of shorthand.

It took him three years, but by the time he was 15 years old he had a working method of reading without sight.

The boy's name was Louis Braille, and the system he invented has been in worldwide use ever since.

It allows blind people to read as fast as sighted people.

In the US today, around 85,000 people are totally blind.

Of those who've learned Braille, 90% are employed.

Of those who haven't only 33% are employed.

Louis Braille took something that was invented for one purpose and turned it into a completely different purpose.

That's two different kinds of creativity.

Mike Greenlees once told me he studied pure math at university.

I said I couldn't do that because I'm no good with numbers.

Mike said pure math wasn't to do with numbers, pure math was more about discovery and abstract thinking – math for its own sake.

Applied math was when someone used these discoveries for a practical purpose.

One type of person discovers something, a different type of person applies it.

And I thought, that could apply to creativity.

Pure creativity would be what you find in art galleries: creativity for its own sake.

Applied creativity would be what we do: creativity with a specific purpose.

We might take a painting, or a sculpture, or a piece of opera and use it to stand out and convey a message.

For us it isn't beauty for its own sake, it has to have a reason.

If it doesn't have a reason, it's just decoration.

Then it's failed at being applied creativity by pretending to be pure creativity.

Applied creativity has to do a job.

Knowing the difference is what makes us effective.

Because nothing that runs in our world should be pure creativity.

Steve Jobs was one of the most creative people in recent years.

But Steve Jobs didn't invent a single thing.

He built the most valuable brand in the world by understanding the difference between pure creativity and applied creativity.

WHY WE WANT COMPLAINTS

In 2007, Apple launched the iPhone.

In America, you could only use the iPhone on AT&T's network.

But a teenager called George Hotz didn't want to use AT&T.

He wanted to use T-Mobile.

So he opened his iPhone, located the processor, scrambled the code, and reprogrammed it to work with any network.

Then he posted a video about it on YouTube, and got two million hits.

Because this was the world's first hacked iPhone.

When he found out about it, Steve Jobs wasn't pleased.

He said: **"This is a constant cat and mouse game we play. People keep trying to break in and it's our job to stop them."**

But Steve Wozniak, co-founder of Apple, didn't see it like that.

He said: **"I understand the mindset of a person who wants to do that, and I don't think of people like that as criminals. In fact, I think that misbehaviour is very strongly correlated with and responsible for creative thought."**

That last line is so good, I'll repeat it.

"Misbehaviour is very strongly correlated with and responsible for creative thought."

In other words, people who are scared stiff of getting into trouble are going to have a hard time being creative.

Creativity is nearly always a reaction against something.

A desire to change things.

That's why it causes outrage.

That's why it goes against the rules.

In 1907, Picasso exhibited his painting 'Les Demoiselles d'Avignon'.

A painting of prostitutes in a brothel.

It combined, for the first time, primitive tribal art with Cubism.

When he saw it, the influential art dealer Ambroise Vollard said: **"This is the work of a mad man."**

The painter Braque said: **"Picasso spits turpentine in our faces."**

But within a year it was considered a game-changing work.

Within a few years, a masterpiece.

Today, it is universally recognised as the painting that marks the birth of modern art.

Ten years later, Marcel Duchamp sent a sculpture for exhibition in New York.

It was simply a urinal with a crude signature.

The committee were horrified, they refused to even have it in the exhibition.

Not only that, but the sculpture was taken outside and destroyed.

Subsequently, that sculpture is seen as the birth of conceptual art.

Real creativity is a reaction against the status quo.

A desire to change things.

If there was no desire to change things, why would you do it?

Especially in our business.

Our business is all about changing things.

And we can't do that unless we get attention.

We have to do that by dominating our environment.

And we won't do that by fitting in, by being quiet and polite.

That's why it's our job to upset people.

To dominate the environment so that we capture the attention everyone's competing for.

What's nice for Duchamp or Picasso is essential for us.

People don't carefully inspect ads the way they look at the exhibits in an art gallery.

If we don't want to rock the boat, we're invisible.

If we're invisible, why are we bothering?

CREATIVITY IS WHATEVER IT TAKES

100 years ago, three out of every four babies born prematurely didn't survive.

This wasn't in underdeveloped countries, this was in Europe and America.

Doctors and nurses did try to save them, but there wasn't a lot they could do.

The little babies weren't fully formed, they were tiny and undernourished.

They couldn't even generate enough heat to warm themselves, so 75% died.

The medical profession accepted that it was the natural way.

Except for Dr Étienne Tarnier, at L'Hôpital Paris Maternité.

He noticed that on farms, chickens' eggs were being hatched by being kept warm.

And in 1880, he and a colleague, Dr Pierre Budin, began trying the same thing on babies.

They had boxes made which would retain the heat, with a glass top to let the light in, and a hot water bottle to keep the tiny body warm.

They were inventing the incubator.

They noticed that the survival rate for these premature babies was much higher.

Obviously the first thing to do was to get these 'incubators' installed in hospitals.

But none of the medical authorities were interested in such a silly, expensive gimmick.

First: they knew it was quite natural for babies born too soon not to survive.

Second: what possible connection could farms and chicken eggs have with humans?

No medical establishment would entertain the idea.

So another colleague, Dr Martin Couney, decided to bypass medical establishments.

He made six incubators and took them to the 1896 World Exhibition in Berlin.

Then he asked the Berlin Charity Hospital for six premature babies.

They gave them to him, as they were almost certain to die anyway.

He hired nurses and exhibited the babies in the incubators, to the public.

The exhibit was called **"Couney's Kinderbrutanstalt"** (Couney's Child Hatchery).

The public paid to see tiny living babies almost a quarter the size of normal babies.

And, against all medical predictions, all six babies survived to grow into healthy infants.

This gave Couney the impetus he needed.

He took his incubators to America, where just as many premature babies were dying.

In 1901 he did the same thing at the Pan American Exhibition in Buffalo, New York.

In 1902, he did it again at the World's Fair.

And in 1903 he moved his exhibit to Coney Island, to Dreamland, and to Luna Park.

He knew people would happily pay 25 cents to see the cutest little babies in the world, wrapped up snug and warm.

And poor families were only too grateful to give their babies a chance to survive.

As a reporter wrote at the time: **"It would be harder to find a finer set of infants anywhere than those which cooed in their mothers' arms while their photographs were being taken yesterday afternoon, or a more satisfied set of paters and maters."**

Couney's incubators exhibited to paying customers at Coney Island for the next 40 years.

During that time they saved 6,500 out of 8,000 premature babies lives.

That's an 85% survival rate, up from a 25% survival rate without the incubators.

Eventually the medical authorities saw sense, and today incubators are saving lives in hospitals worldwide.

All because those rebellious doctors didn't listen to conventional wisdom.

Conventional wisdom says you can't question people in authority.

But those rebellious doctors knew they were right, so they did whatever it took.

If they couldn't save lives in a hospital, they'd save lives in a fairground.

Even if they had to charge people 25 cents a time to see them do it.

There's an old Chinese saying: **"Those that say it can't be done, shouldn't get in the way of those that are doing it."**

SPINNING A YARN

Scotland is unique in that each family has its own patterned cloth called a tartan.

Each tartan is different and each family, or clan, can trace its heritage back a thousand years to the particular pattern it's always worn.

Except they can't.

It was all made up in 1829 by two brothers from Surrey.

Tartan patterns always existed of course, but they had nothing to do with clans.

It was just whatever cloth was available to the people of a particular region.

The oldest example is in the National Museum of Scotland in Edinburgh: a small scrap of wool, herringbone, tweedy cloth from around 300 AD.

But it had no meaning, different highlanders wore whatever cloth was available in their area, naturally people in different areas wove differing patterns.

And over the years tartan came to be known as a particularly Scottish highland cloth.

Then, in 1822, the theatrical King George IV paid a state visit to Edinburgh.

He wanted to see tartan everywhere, as his fantasy of Scotland.

So suddenly every family wanted to own a tartan.

Seeing an opportunity, two brothers from Godalming in Surrey jumped at it.

They were born John and Charles Allen in Wales, but changed their name to the more Scottish sounding Allan, then Hay Allan, then Hay, then finally Sobieski Stuart.

They published a book called *Vestiarium Scoticum*.

They said this book was copied from a document from 1721, which was itself a copy of a parchment from 1571, detailing the tartans worn by 75 different clans, from the highlands, the lowlands, and the borders.

The book, and the brothers, were received with open arms by Scots nobility.

It meant everyone could tell exactly what tartan they were entitled to, and could proudly boast of their heritage by wearing it to formal gatherings.

The brothers were the toast of Scottish aristocracy, they were given wealth and land.

But not everyone was convinced.

One of the most famous Scotsmen, Sir Walter Scott, wrote that the book **"sounded like a tartan weaver trying to drum up trade"** and that **"the idea of distinguishing clans by tartan is but a fashion of modern date"** and that **"no lowlander ever wore a clan tartan"**.

But in 1832 Sir Walter Scott died and, with him out of the way, the brothers were able to release another book *Costumes of the Clans* and, in 1847, *The Tales of the Century*, in which they claimed to be the grandsons of Bonnie Prince Charlie.

Eventually, in 1895, the *Glasgow Herald* tracked down the supposed 1721 copy of the *Vestiarium Scoticum*.

Their chemist wrote: **"The document bore evidence of having been treated with some chemical agents to give the writing a more aged appearance than it is entitled to."**

So, proof that it was a fake.

But none of that affected the 'tradition' that the Sobieski Stuart brothers had started.

Even today, people with Scots ancestry come from all over the world to have their 'clan tartan' made into a kilt in Edinburgh.

The need for a sense of belonging overrides facts and makes truth irrelevant.

As David Hume, another Scotsman, said: **"Reason is the slave of the passions"**.

Which is a great lesson for us, and worth remembering.

Sometimes the answer lies in the product, sometimes the answer lies in the consumer.

And sometimes the consumer is more important than the product.

And an exciting lie is nearly always more attractive than a boring truth.

WHEN WEAKNESS IS STRENGTH

Like everywhere else, Israel is split.

In their case it's between the ultra-religious and the secular-modernisers.

The ultra-orthodox have similar views to fundamentalists in most religions.

They won't let their followers watch films, the internet, or mix with the secular.

Every Saturday groups of these men protest in the centre of Jerusalem.

In the middle of these protests is a café called Bastet, owned by Klil Lifshitz.

Klil herself is two things the ultra-orthodox hate, she's secular and a lesbian.

Her café is full of more things they hate, it's vegan and LGBT friendly, and it's staffed by women who are feminists.

So every weekend Klil gets noisy demonstrations marching past her café.

In 2019, the Eurovision Song Contest was held in Tel Aviv, a more liberal city.

But the work to prepare for the event was being done on Saturday, during the day.

The Chief Rabbi called for Shabbat to be extended 20 minutes due to "the great desecration".

No one in liberal Tel Aviv was very bothered, but in Jerusalem the ultra-orthodox protest became angrier and noisier than ever.

Dozens of furious men blocking the streets and stopping traffic.

The centre of Jerusalem was shut down.

The police were called to clear the disruption, but the protestors fought with them.

The protestors were as big and tough as the cops, and there were more of them.

They attacked the police, who were being overpowered.

Which is when a really creative thing happened.

A small thing that transformed everything and changed the entire game.

Something so creative, no one saw it coming.

Klil and her staff of waitresses came out of the café and onto the street.

They lifted up their T-shirts and they took them off.

Then they jumped up and down waving them above their heads exposing their brassieres to the protestors.

All the big, fierce, violent rioters stopped dead.

They covered their eyes, they turned their heads, and they ran away as fast as they could.

Their ultra-orthodox religion didn't allow them to look on women who were **"immodestly dressed"**.

They couldn't do anything but run away.

The women carried on jumping up and down, waving their tops in the air and showing their brassieres, until the rioters had disappeared.

The situation had been reversed, not by opposing force with force, but by out-thinking it.

By looking for a weak point upstream of that force.

That's real creativity.

And since that day something else has happened, the weekly protest marches have avoided Klil's café.

It seems the ultra-orthodox can't risk being exposed to women **"dressed immodestly"**.

That's a brilliant lesson in not letting the competition write your agenda.

Sometimes what you perceive as your weakness can actually be your strength.

That's how Bill Bernbach revolutionised advertising with campaigns for VW and Avis.

That's what Mary Wells did for Benson & Hedges.

That's what Carl Ally did for Federal Express.

That's what John Webster did for Cadbury's Smash.

Sometimes the strongest thing you've got isn't a traditional strength at all.

Sometimes the strongest thing you've got is a perceived weakness.

PLUS ÇA CHANGE...

Theophilus Van Kannel was born in Philadelphia in 1841.

He was born into a wealthy family, his mother held regular salons.

At these, all the other mothers liked to display their well brought up offspring.

This was awkward for her because Theophilus refused to obey rules.

Chivalry for instance, made no sense to him.

He didn't see why he should hold a door open for women who were perfectly capable of opening the door themselves.

This behaviour embarrassed his mother so much that she spanked him in front of all the other mothers and daughters.

Which, or course, just made Theophilus more determined to overturn that rule.

Especially when he later married a woman who, he found out, put a premium on chivalry.

She expected him to open every door in the house whenever she wished to pass through.

One morning, Theophilus stormed out of the bedroom, saying:

"All this opening doors twaddle just will not do. I cannot be rushing around my own house to usher you from room to room! You are a grown woman and can locomote perfectly well on your own."

But his wife, Abigail, was just as strong-willed, and when he returned home that evening she was still sitting in the bedroom in the exact spot where he left her.

Something had to be done about this problem of opening doors for women.

So for the next three years he set about solving the problem.

It cost him $9,837 (a quarter of a million in today's dollars) but in 1888 he received US Patent 387,571 for his **'Storm Door Structure'**.

It was actually the world's first revolving door.

It was the solution to his problem, because it was actually now more chivalrous for a man to go through first so he could push the door for a lady to follow.

Consequently, he had 14 of these doors fitted in his and his mother's homes.

He was so pleased with the results, he decided to market the door.

But of course, he had to sell it to the public as a logical improvement.

So he wrote in a sales pamphlet: **"This door prevents a direct path between the interior and exterior of a structure, making it useful as a partial airlock, minimizing heat-loss."**

And he carefully laid out all the selling points:

1. It is perfectly noiseless.

2. It effectually prevents the entrance of snow, rain, or dust.

3. It cannot be blown open by the wind.

4. It excludes street noise.

5. Persons can pass both in and out at the same time.

The original advertising slogan was: **"The Door That is Always Closed"**.

In the language of the day it was advertised as preventing the entrance of "noxious effluvia" and "baleful miasmas".

The first commercial use of the revolving door was in 1899 at Rector's restaurant, in Times Square between 43rd and 44th Streets.

Today revolving doors are used on practically every office building in the world.

The irony is that gentlemen will still let ladies go first.

So however much Theophilus Van Kannel revolutionised doors, he didn't change the behaviour that was the original reason for his invention.

What can we, in a time of constant technological innovation, learn from that?

Well, as Bill Bernbach said: **"It took millions of years for man's instincts to develop.**

It will take millions more for them to even vary.

It is fashionable to talk about changing man.

A communicator must be concerned with unchanging man."

IN THE BEGINNING WAS THE WORD

In 1967, John Lennon had left his wife and son and was living with Yoko Ono.

Paul McCartney didn't want Cynthia Lennon to think he'd also abandoned her and Julian, just because John had left, so he drove to see them in Weybridge.

Being a songwriter, he naturally began making up a tune as he drove.

He hoped Julian wouldn't start crying, that would just make a sad situation worse.

So he sang: **"Hey Jules, don't make it bad. Take a sad song and make it better."**

In the event, although he liked the song, he thought 'Jules' was a bit awkward to sing.

So he changed the name to Jude, and the song became **'Hey Jude'**.

The Beatles recorded it and it was released in 1968.

At the same time, they'd just opened a fashion boutique, named Apple, in Baker Street.

McCartney was proud of his new song and put the title across the window: **HEY JUDE**.

He thought it was a great opportunity, with all the people and buses going by.

Which is when he found out that his reality wasn't everyone's reality.

He got a phone call, an elderly man was on the line, his voice breaking in anger.

The man shouted: **"What do you mean? How dare you? Take it down. Take it down."**

McCartney tried to ask him what was the matter.

The man shouted: **"Jude! Jude! Jude! Haven't we had enough of this? I'm going to send my son round to beat you up."**

The man's name was Mr Leon and he had a heavy accent, eventually McCartney was able to work out the problem: the word 'Jude' meant Jew in German.

This was a Jewish man who had escaped Nazi Germany where Jewish shops had **JUDE** painted in large letters in whitewash on their windows.

All over the country, **JUDEN RAUS** (Jews Out) was painted on walls and windows.

Joseph Goebbels made a propaganda film that was shown to everyone: **'DER EWIGE JUDE'** (The Eternal Jew).

Over footage of rats scuttling about, the Nazi voice-over said:

"Where rats appear, they bring ruin by destroying mankind's goods and foodstuffs. In this way, they spread disease, plague, leprosy, typhoid fever, cholera, dysentery, and so on. They are cunning, cowardly, and cruel and are found mostly in large packs. Among the animals, they represent the rudiment of an insidious, underground destruction – just like the Jews among human beings."

This was the world that Mr Leon had escaped, and this is what **HEY JUDE** in a shop window looked like to him.

To us, the war seems like ancient history, but 1968 was only 23 years after the war.

To give it perspective, it's 2020 now, 23 years ago was 1997, it would be recent history.

Of course, McCartney apologised, immediately took the words out of the window and persuaded the man that he meant no harm.

It's interesting that his reality wasn't Mr Leon's reality.

Paul McCartney was the musician of the Beatles, John Lennon was the lyricist, and John Lennon read something completely different into the words of Hey Jude.

Lennon said the line: **"Now that you've found her, go out and get her"** was actually Paul saying it was okay for him to leave his wife and child and go off with Yoko.

Which shows that words are received, and interpreted, strictly through the filter of the listener's situation and experience.

And that's why we have to be responsible not just for speaking correctly, but for being heard correctly.

As the man who invented semiotics, Ferdinand de Saussure, said: **"Everyone, left to his own devices, forms an idea about what goes on in language, which is very far from the truth."**

If we don't take strict control of our own communications, someone else will.

PART 3

IGNORANCE IS A SECRET WEAPON

GIVE 'EM WHAT THEY WANT

Before the war, people from London's East End didn't have holidays as we know them today.

Two weeks off, doing nothing.

They couldn't afford it, if they didn't work they didn't get paid.

So the nearest they got to a holiday was to go hop picking.

They jumped in a lorry which took them to the hop fields.

Then they spent two weeks in Kent getting paid for picking hops.

They loved it because they were in the country, in the sun and the open air.

They got away from the East End and the grime and the routine.

To them it was like a holiday.

But after the war, things changed for the working class.

Your employer had to give you two weeks' PAID holiday a year.

Ordinary people had two weeks off, doing nothing.

This was a new concept for the working class, they'd never had time off doing nothing.

They weren't like the middle class who knew how to enjoy leisure time: reading books, going to concerts, visiting museums, art galleries, historical or cultural sites.

The working class didn't know what to do.

Which is where a man called Billy Butlin came in.

Billy Butlin had been a fairground owner before the war, so he knew how the working class spent their leisure time.

He recognised several things were happening at once that could be brought together:

1. The working class had two weeks off, and they didn't know where to go or what to do.

2. They had the money to pay for somewhere to stay.

3. With the war being over, the army was being disbanded and army camps were becoming empty all over Britain.

And Billy Butlin put these three things together.

He bought up empty army camps for less than half what they were worth.

He turned them into holiday camps.

He put entertainment into each of these camps: swimming pools, dancing, bingo, fairground rides, silly competitions.

And then he launched a new lifestyle concept using simple logic that anyone could understand:

"A WEEK'S HOLIDAY FOR A WEEK'S PAY."

Everyone could understand that, everyone could see how it made sense.

It sounded like a fair deal, a straight swap.

You swap a week's wages for a week's holiday.

Who wouldn't want that?

And Billy Butlin's understanding of what the working class wanted worked.

To make sure they didn't have a chance to get bored, he even hired people whose job it was to keep them entertained at all times, he called them Redcoats.

Which itself became a training for professional entertainers.

People like: Benny Hill, Des O'Connor, Cliff Richard, Jimmy Tarbuck.

They trained to entertain the working class, so they knew what the working class wanted.

And they all became very successful, as did Butlin's.

At its height, a million ordinary people a year visited Butlin's.

There's a lot of money in knowing what ordinary people want.

EXPERTS

My dad was an old-fashioned copper.

Many, many years ago he was called to a dead body, upstairs in a boarding house.

The body was laying on its back in the middle of the room.

No carpet, just floorboards, hardly any furniture.

Dad had seen a lot of dead bodies but this one didn't look quite right.

It wasn't in a natural position for someone who had just collapsed.

It looked artificially arranged.

But he couldn't touch it until the Medical Examiner arrived, so he waited.

Eventually the Examiner turned up, clearly in a bad mood.

Dad said: **"Here's the body sir."**

The Examiner said: **"Thank you Sergeant, I can recognise a dead body on my own."**

So Dad kept his thoughts to himself.

The Examiner checked for a pulse, and started writing out a certificate.

Dad said: **"Don't you want us to turn him over sir, so you can get a better look?"**

The Examiner huffed and said: **"Sergeant, are you a doctor?"**

Dad said: **"No sir."**

The Examiner said: **"Well I am, and I can recognise a heart attack when I see one."**

And he carried on writing out the certificate saying that the man died of a heart attack.

Finally he said: **"Now the examination is complete, you may remove the body."**

And he turned to leave.

Dad and the constable turned the body over.

As the Examiner was going through the door, Dad said: **"Er, excuse me sir."**

The Examiner rolled his eyes and exhaled: **"What is it now, Sergeant?"**

Dad started counting.

He said: **"This bloke's got one, two, three, four, five, six, seven stab wounds in his back sir."**

The Examiner said: **"WHAT?"**

Dad said: **"I thought that position didn't look natural."**

The Examiner said: **"But there's no blood on the floor."**

Dad said: **"No sir, it looks like he was killed somewhere else and moved here. I thought the position looked a bit funny."**

The Examiner said: **"Well you might have said something, Sergeant."**

Dad swallowed and didn't answer.

But he did learn something about experts.

They know everything about everything and never need to listen to anyone else.

And if it ever goes wrong it's never their fault.

Like Dad said, what's the point arguing: an ordinary copper against a Medical Examiner?

But that lesson did rub off on me.

I learned that experts actually don't have any more brains than the rest of us.

They certainly don't know everything.

That knowledge gives us freedom.

As Steve Jobs said: **"The great lesson in life is that everything you see around you was made up by people who were no smarter than you. And you can change it."**

Or, as the newspaper tycoon, William Randolph Hearst, said: **"I don't hire experts to tell me what to do. I hire experts to tell me how to do what I want to do."**

That's the important thing for us to learn about experts.

Whether in marketing, technology, new media, strategy, semiotics, whatever.

They may be experts in what they do, but they're not experts in what we do.

WE ALL USE SEMIOTICS ALL THE TIME

One of the most influential games of football happened in 1966.

It wasn't the final, but it was the World Cup and it did feature England.

It was the quarter-final against Argentina.

The referee was German, Rudolf Kreitlein, and he gave a foul against Argentina.

The Argentine captain, Antonio Rattín, didn't agree.

In fact he didn't agree very loudly.

He shouted and gesticulated in an angry, threatening manner.

This may have been standard behaviour in Argentina, but the German referee didn't speak Spanish and he wasn't having any of it.

So he sent Rattín off.

But Rattín didn't understand, he didn't speak German and refused to go.

He was upset that he couldn't express himself to the referee, the referee was upset that a player wouldn't do what he was told.

The argument dragged on for eight minutes, until Rattín was eventually persuaded to leave the field and play was resumed.

The next day the papers were full of it, plus the fact that both Jack and Bobby Charlton had been booked in that match.

This was news to the Charlton brothers, no one had told them.

They called FIFA to clarify the situation, it turned out that Jack had been booked but not Bobby.

So the referee thought one thing, the press thought something else, and the players themselves thought something completely different.

Combined with the row with the Argentine captain this was clearly a mess.

How could you play world-class international football when the referee couldn't make himself understood to the players?

In short how could you transcend the problem of different languages?

Ken Aston was in charge of all referees for the 1966 World Cup and this was the problem he was faced with.

How to communicate clearly to everyone what was happening when they all spoke different languages?

This was going through his mind as he drove from Wembley to Lancaster Gate.

He drove up to a set of traffic lights in Kensington High Street.

As he approached them they turned yellow, so he slowed down.

When he got close they went red, so he stopped.

Then something in his brain went ping.

He thought, everyone understands traffic lights in every language: yellow for: **'Be careful, slow down'** – red for: **'Stop, that's it'.**

When he got home he explained it to his wife, Hilda.

She straight away cut two pieces of card in the different colours, just big enough to fit into his shirt pocket.

Now, without saying a word, a referee could pull out a red or yellow card and everyone watching – players, fans, journalists – would know what had just happened.

Even without anyone saying anything, there couldn't be any confusion.

That is *real* semiotics: communication without words.

And it works all over the world in every game of football played every day.

And it didn't take a department of people with degrees to work it out.

All it took was someone thinking the way ordinary people think.

That, and about thirty seconds of common sense.

As Bill Bernbach said, **"Our proper area of study is simple, timeless, human truths."**

ADVERTISING ISN'T MEDICINE

In 1896, the Missouri, Kansas and Texas Railroad, known as the 'KT' (or Katy) for short, was in financial trouble.

William Crush was responsible for attracting passengers and freight, he needed to increase sales and awareness, fast.

But in Texas in 1896, there was no media to advertise in: no movies, no TV, no radio.

So Crush needed to come up with a way to do two things in a hurry:

1. Get a lot of free publicity for the Katy.

2. Get people to quickly spend a lot more money on railroad tickets.

He grew up in Iowa along the railway tracks and as a boy often wondered what would happen if two trains ran into each other:

"I believed that somewhere in the makeup of every normal person there lurks the suppressed desire to smash things up. So I was convinced that thousands of others would be just as curious as I was to see what actually would take place when two speeding locomotives came together."

And that was his plan: two obsolete 35-ton steam trains crashing head on into each other at 50 mph, a combined speed of 100 mph.

Of course, he couldn't say that, he had to call it a **"scientific experiment designed to study railroad safety"**.

The management of the Katy built several miles of track 15 miles north of Waco, Texas.

Entry was free, but there were no roads, the only way to get there was by train.

Fares from across Texas were priced at $2.00 from Austin, up to $3.50 from Houston (that's $60 and $105 in today's money).

If the predicted 20,000 people travelled to see it, the Katy would make a lot of money.

In the event, 40,000 turned up and the event was a massive success.

Well almost.

One reporter wrote of the crash: **"The immense crowd was paralyzed with apprehension.**

There was a swift instance of silence, and then, as if controlled by a single impulse, both boilers exploded simultaneously and the air was filled with flying missiles of iron and steel varying in size from a postage stamp to half a driving wheel."

A Civil War veteran who was there said it was more terrifying than the Battle of Gettysburg.

Three people were killed and dozens were maimed.

Photographer Jarvis Deane was struck in the eye by a bolt, and blinded.

(Doctors said he was lucky, the bolt snagged on his eye socket preventing it from becoming lodged in his brain.)

As you'd expect, the management of the Katy fired William Crush immediately.

But then a strange thing happened.

The train crash made a massive profit and was covered by every newspaper in America.

Suddenly the Katy was the most famous railroad in the USA.

So, the next day they hired William Crush back.

In fact, New York, Chicago, and Minneapolis now wanted their own train crashes.

It seemed America couldn't get enough head-on locomotive wrecks.

In fact, until the 1930s, crashing railroad trains became one of the biggest entertainments in the US, with over 146 train wrecks.

We may look down our noses at train wrecks as a popular form of entertainment.

And as far as train wrecks for advertising, what even is the brand purpose?

But for four decades train wrecks were amazingly successful.

Because people don't want to be lectured about what they should like.

People don't want advertising administered like taking medicine.

People just want fun.

FARMING BY THE SEAT OF YOUR PANTS

Farmers aren't scientists.

They work long, hard hours outside in all conditions. It's tough manual labour.

They don't have white coats and laboratory equipment.

So, analysing the fertility of their soil can be a slow and costly process to undertake.

But knowing the fertility of their fields is crucial.

Because that's where everything either grows, or it doesn't.

That's what is really creative about the Canadian Soil Association's initiative.

They showed farmers how to test their soil for fertility, quickly and cheaply.

All they need is a pair of dirty cotton underpants.

When they've worn them for a while, bury them in a field and wait two months.

After two months dig them up.

If they're full of holes and disintegrating it means the soil is healthy and organically thriving, great for crops.

But if they're still in the same state they were when they buried them, it means the soil is poor quality and not good for crops.

Organically thriving soil needs to be full of microbes and bacteria, fungi, protozoa, nematodes, anthropoids, earthworms.

These will make short work of a pair of cotton underpants.

If the underpants aren't eaten away, it means the soil has none of this activity.

Therefore, it doesn't have sufficient nutrients for healthy plant life.

Farmers in California and Canada began spreading the word about this simple test.

They called it **#soilmyundies**.

It became amazingly popular and it spread to the UK, Australia, and New Zealand.

Farmers can plant dozens of pairs of underpants all over their farms, in different areas of different fields.

They need to know whether the soil is too dry, too wet, too acidic, too alkaline, over-worked, lacking nutrients, or low in other organic matter.

Then they can work out how to treat their soil in order to improve it.

Evan Wiig, Executive Director of the California Farmers' Guild, said: **"Cotton is an organic material and breaks down naturally just like anything else you'd put on your compost pile.**

So, if you bury cotton in soil teeming with life, all those creatures will begin to feast on it.

If you have dead soil, if it is totally lifeless, you should be able to pull the underpants out of the ground, throw them in the washing machine and put them on like nothing happened. But if you have healthy soil you should have nothing left but an elastic waistband."

Fertile soil isn't just crucial for crop farmers.

Cattle farmers or sheep farmers need lots of lush healthy grass for their grazing herds.

That's why #soilmyundies caught on with farmers all over the world.

Hard-working people who need a fast, simple answer they can do something about.

And word has spread throughout the international press as well as the farming press.

The learning for us is what made it catch on, how did it go viral?

The truth is, the test will work just as well with anything that's 100% cotton.

Whether it's a T-shirt, a T-towel, a pair of socks, or just any piece of cloth.

It doesn't have to be underpants.

But calling it a name like #cottonsoilchallenge just wouldn't have caught on.

It doesn't sound cheeky and rude, it doesn't sound fun, like **#soilmyundies**.

The test would work with anything cotton, but it wouldn't get as much press.

It wouldn't make people laugh, so it wouldn't go viral.

As Walt Disney said, **"We have to entertain in order to educate, because the other way round doesn't work."**

GRANDMA KNOWS BEST

Joe Scaravella lived in Brooklyn.

In just one year, he lost his grandmother, his mother, and his sister.

To escape the sad memories he moved to Staten Island.

While walking he noticed a vacant shop on the main street, and several things came together in Joe's mind.

First – although he couldn't cook, being Italian, he'd always wanted to own and run a restaurant.

Second – most restaurants claim to be **'artisanal'**, even though this actually means young bearded chefs who'd only read about artisanal traditions.

Third – Joe missed the strong powerful women in his life.

So putting all these thoughts together gave Joe an idea.

What if he opened a restaurant that was genuinely artisanal, not just in theory?

What if he could find genuine Italian grandmas, like his own, to come and cook?

Those grandmas (**'nonna'** in Italian) wouldn't have learned recipes from books.

They'd have learned it from their mothers, who learned it from their mothers, and so on going back generations.

Joe knew there were Italian nonnas like this living in Brooklyn.

They'd spent their lives cooking for their husbands, who were now dead, and their children, who'd grown up and left home.

So these nonnas had no one to cook for.

Giving them a job, cooking their traditional dishes, would give them a new lease of life.

So Joe opened **'Enoteca Maria'** (named after his mother) in 2006 and it was an immediate success.

It served a different sort of food than any other Italian restaurant.

It was the traditional food of poor people: sheep's head, liver, hearts, gizzards, food you couldn't get anywhere else.

Then one day in 2015, it occurred to Joe that there were many grandmothers from all over the world in New York, not just Italian.

And Joe began expanding the restaurant to offer traditional food from different grandmas.

One nonna would always be Italian, but the other would be a different country each night.

So Monday – Pakistan, Tuesday – Sri Lanka, Wednesday – Philippines, Thursday – Armenia, Friday – Russia, and so on.

Always with a choice of traditional Italian food if you preferred.

But these recipes would be what you couldn't get anywhere else, genuine folk food cooked by the people who grew up with recipes that couldn't be found in any cookbook.

And the grandmas love it.

They get to meet and swap recipes with different grandmas from all over the world.

They get to cook their food for a restaurant full of people who love to eat it.

And the people come back again and again, because every night Joe's restaurant is a different restaurant: Polish, Nigerian, Syrian, Columbian, Greek, Argentinian, Czech, Ecuadorian, Dominican, Algerian, Liberian.

And every night Joe's restaurant is packed.

He can't believe it, he has people booking from London, Sydney, and Paris before they even get to New York.

And Joe can't believe people get on the Staten Island Ferry to come to his restaurant.

Like he says, you have Manhattan right there: 24,457 eating places of which 7,995 are rated amongst the best restaurants in the world.

Why would anyone get on the ferry to come to a restaurant in Staten Island?

The answer is what works in advertising and everywhere else.

The answer is, Joe's restaurant is different, and that's what works.

WHO PUT THAT THERE?

In Ridley Scott's film *1492: Conquest of Paradise* we are shown Columbus watching a ship disappear over the horizon and speculating that the world might be round.

Before Columbus, apparently, most people thought the world was flat.

Obviously this isn't true.

If it was, why would anyone finance an expedition for him to sail off the edge of the world?

No, people had known for centuries that the world was round.

But that was about all they did know, everything else was guesswork.

In those days, the sole reason for exploration was trade and profit.

And the most profitable place to trade was the Far East, for spices and silks.

So, the overland Spice Route, via Constantinople, had been the traditional route.

But Constantinople had fallen to the Moslems in 1453.

So an alternative had to be found.

Portugal was the most powerful country in the world, and they began to explore sea routes to the Far East.

In 1488, Bartolomeu Dias sailed the length of Africa and round the Cape of Good Hope.

Meanwhile, King Ferdinand of Aragon had recently married Queen Isabella of Castile.

They unified their two countries and created Spain.

They were interested in finding a better sea route than the Portuguese.

That's how Columbus persuaded them to sail west – to cross the Atlantic to reach the Far East.

They thought there was nothing in the way but ocean.

They gave their approval for a simple reason, Columbus got his sums wrong.

Of course, he didn't know America was in the way, no one did.

But more than that, Columbus thought the world was smaller than it was.

According to Columbus, the circumference of the world was 25,000 nautical miles, instead of the 40,000 it actually is.

So Columbus calculated the distance from the Canary Islands to Japan as 2,000 nautical miles, instead of the 10,000 it actually is.

It's five times further away than he allowed for.

If he'd tried to sail the actual distance without landfall, his entire crew would have died from thirst and starvation before he was half way.

So Columbus's ignorance saved him.

But the ignorance didn't end there.

Because Columbus never landed in America he never knew the mainland was there.

In 1492 he landed in a group of islands, in what today is called the West Indies.

They're called the West Indies because that's where Columbus thought he was, Indonesia and Malaysia.

He thought he'd reached the Far East.

In 1494, to settle disputes between the two superpowers, the Pope drew a North-South line 270 leagues west of Cape Verde.

He gave all land to the west of that (Africa, India, China) to Spain.

He gave all land east of that (what he thought was the new world) to Portugal.

Six years later, Pedro Álvares Cabral discovered Brazil, which no one knew about.

The Pope's line actually cut South America in half, which is why today Brazil speaks Portuguese, and everyone else speaks Spanish.

Several years after Columbus, in 1502, Amerigo Vespucci landed on the mainland.

He discovered the continent itself – which is why it's named America and not Columbia.

Columbus died believing he had discovered a new route to India and China.

He never knew he had discovered nearly a third of the world's land mass.

And that is the power, and the value, of ignorance.

WHY SIMPLE IS SMARTER

If we're any good at all we want our work to 'go viral'.

That's what we used to call 'getting into the language' or 'word of mouth'.

Today it's also known as 'earned media'.

(There being three types of media: bought media, owned media, and earned media.)

Earned media is media we create for free: by getting people to use it in daily speech.

If we can do that we've created free media and magnified our budget many times.

Every time someone repeats it, it's media we haven't paid for.

How we do this is by creating something people want to repeat, something fun or useful.

There is a belief that the only way anything goes viral is in so-called 'viral media': YouTube, Facebook, social media, on the internet.

But this isn't true, every day 99% of what is put up on the internet disappears.

What's true is what's always been true, things people love go viral.

If we want to learn how to do it let's look at some of the expressions that have 'gone viral' and passed into everyday usage, take the following:

"Out of the frying pan into the fire"

"There's no point closing the barn door after the horse has bolted"

"Every man for himself"

"Don't put the cart before the horse"

"Half a loaf is better than none"

"Every dog has its day"

"You can lead a horse to water but you can't make it drink"

We can all agree those expressions went viral without the need for technology.

In fact they were written by a man who was born about the time America was being discovered, and died just before the Spanish Armada, before the internet, before electricity, around the time of the first printing press.

His name was John Heywood and he was born in 1497 and died in 1580.

He wasn't a famous playwright, as Shakespeare became, he was mainly a performer.

But he used to write his own simple plays to incorporate his singing, dancing, and juggling.

In Henry VIII's court records he was listed as a "Synger" and paid 100 shillings a quarter.

The writing was just an excuse for the performance, so he kept it simple and catchy.

Simple and catchy is what ordinary people like, so his writing has stayed viral, stayed in the language for 500 years.

See if you can recognise these in their 1542 form:

"Haste maketh waste"

"Out of sight out of mind"

"Look ere ye leap"

"Two heads are better than one"

"Beggars should be no choosers"

"I know on which side my bread is buttered"

"One good turn asketh another"

"A penny for your thought"

"Rome was not built in one day"

"This hitteth the nail on the head"

"Better late than never"

"The more the merrier"

"You cannot see the wood for the trees"

"Wolde ye both eate your cake and have your cake?"

Maybe if we could stop our obsession with technology and complexity, we could learn to write stuff like that, stuff that catches on with ordinary people.

Stuff that goes viral, instead of stuff that disappears the moment it runs.

PROPAGANDA IS ADVERTISING

At school, we were all taught about the Armada.

In 1588, a massive fleet of Spanish ships tried to invade England.

They were to bring a huge army across from the Netherlands.

The Spanish fleet anchored overnight at Calais, but the English sent in fire ships.

These were the equivalent of guided missiles: unmanned ships full of blazing pitch, brimstone, gunpowder, and tar.

The wind and tide carried them straight into the middle of the anchored Spanish fleet.

The thing sailors on wooden ships feared more than anything was fire, they didn't have time to raise their anchors, so they cut their anchor cables just to escape.

Because of the wind, they couldn't go back down the English Channel, so they tried to escape around Scotland and Ireland, but then vicious storms blew up.

The Spanish couldn't use their anchors to stop them getting blown onto the rocks, so a lot of their ships were wrecked, and then looted.

5,000 men were killed by drowning, or slaughtered by the local Scots and Irish.

The remains of the fleet limped back to Spain, and that was the end of Spanish sea power.

At least, that's what we were taught at school.

We were never taught what happened the very next year, 1589.

That's when an English fleet tried the same thing in reverse.

The English tried to invade Spain with a fleet as big as the Spanish Armada had been.

The results were very similar to those the Spanish experienced.

Compare the two Armadas:

In 1588 the Spanish had 130 ships, in 1589 the English had 150 ships.

In 1588 the Spanish had 26,000 men, in 1589 the English had 23,000 men.

In 1588 the Spanish lost 11,000 dead, in 1589 the English lost 19,000 dead.

In 1588 the Spanish lost 63 ships, in 1589 the English lost 58 ships.

We were never taught about that at school, because it isn't part of English history.

History is mainly propaganda, which is another word for advertising.

In propaganda, like advertising, you want your product to look good, so you only mention the good bits, not the bad bits.

The English have always been very good at propaganda.

The six main historical victories, every schoolchild knows, are: The Battle of Hastings, Agincourt, the Spanish Armada, Waterloo, Dunkirk, and Alamein.

The thing is that two of these were actually defeats: The Battle of Hastings, and Dunkirk.

But they aren't taught as defeats.

This is what Bill Bernbach taught us about advertising.

How to turn a negative into a positive.

The other interesting thing is that the Spanish didn't publicise the English defeat in 1589, as the English had publicised the Spanish defeat the previous year.

This is because, at that time, Spain ruled the world.

They were, in effect, market leader and only interested in growing the market: expanding into new territories across the Atlantic in the New World.

England was just a challenger brand, and Spain didn't need to compete by trying to take share from them.

But because England was a smaller brand, their attention was on taking share from the bigger brand: Spain.

So England publicised the Spanish loss in 1588 as much as possible.

Thereby elevating England, in everyone's mind, to a competitor with the market leader.

Which it soon was, and eventually became market leader itself.

Proving that propaganda (like advertising) can be more powerful than the truth.

TINNED MEAT

The First World War, unlike the Second, was fought in a very small area.

400 miles of trenches and both sides shelling each other with everything they had.

So, after a few years the land was a deep, muddy, gluey porridge.

And there was so much barbed wire, you couldn't see where it began and ended.

No wonder neither side could move.

The British thought they'd invented a way around this: the tank.

A pill box with tracks on, that could move over mud and barbed wire.

It was crude and primitive, basically just a metal room with an engine inside.

It took a crew of nine to work it and it moved as slowly as walking.

One of the early uses was at Passchendaele in 1917.

In command of one particular tank was Captain Donald Richardson.

Driving was his second in command, Lieutenant George Hill.

As shells hit the side of the tank, pieces of metal broke away and spun through the air like razor blades.

One of these hit Hill, he slumped forward over the throttle, the tank slid into a shell crater and stuck there.

Private Brady opened the door to get out and try to free the tank, but he was shot dead.

Private Trew tried to follow him, but was hit by shrapnel from inside the tank.

As the Germans attacked, the crew used rifles and pistols through the slits to fight them off.

They held off German attacks all day and night.

The next day Private Arthurs was hit by shrapnel from inside the tank.

Then a German threw a grenade in through a slit, Captain Richardson shot the man and Private Morrey threw it back before it exploded.

They held on a second day but, as well as the Germans, the British were starting to shell the tank, not wanting it to be captured.

Sergeant Missen volunteered to crawl back through no man's land to tell the British there were still soldiers alive inside it.

They had no water, so by the second day they were drinking water from the engine's radiator.

Private Morrey and Lance Corporal Binley were both hit by shrapnel from inside the tank.

By the third day, the crew had run out of ammunition, no one was coming to get them, it became obvious they'd have to try to get back to their own lines.

So in the dark, they began crawling through the mud and the wire and the dead bodies.

Amazingly, eight out of the original nine crew members made it back alive.

But none of that is my favourite part of the story.

My favourite part of the story is what they named their tank before the attack.

Painted on the side, in big letters, was the name FRAY BENTOS.

Now for anyone who doesn't know, Fray Bentos was the brand of tinned meat for the working class: corned beef, and steak & kidney pies.

Cheap but long-lasting meat that was also the main army meat ration, named after the town of Fray Bentos in Uruguay where the packing plant was.

What I love is the humour of the men in the tank.

They didn't call their tank: VICTORY, or LIBERTY, or FREEDOM, or what we'd now call a **'brand purpose'**.

They wanted a laugh, so they named it after meat in a tin, which was what they felt like.

They just wanted a laugh, which is something marketing experts can't understand.

Ordinary people don't want a pompous brand purpose, they want a laugh.

They ignore pompous brand purpose, but gratefully include a laugh into their lives.

If we're having a laugh it makes the world a little bit better, it helps us keep a sense of perspective.

Which may be why the crew of FRAY BENTOS became the most highly decorated tank crew of the entire war.

PART 4

SIMPLE IS SMART. COMPLICATED IS STUPID.

A GOOD IDEA DOESN'T CARE WHO HAS IT

In 1879, a Scotsman, James Murray, began to compile the *Oxford English Dictionary*.

The project was simple but vast: to list every single word in the English language.

Not just the top few thousand, but absolutely every word, however obscure.

And not just the meaning, but when it first appeared and when it was modified.

This was an insane project, almost beyond comprehension.

It meant reading every book ever published in English, every word however esoteric.

The problem was they could never afford the enormous amount of manpower needed.

So, in 1879, James Murray invented crowdsourcing.

He printed a four-page leaflet appealing for volunteer readers.

He sent it to newspapers and magazines in Britain, America, and the colonies.

He even sent it to bookshops to insert in books, and to display on their counters.

He asked readers to note words, what they meant and where they'd first appeared.

He was inundated with replies, eventually six million contributions.

The work took forever (eventually seventy years). Every letter took several years.

James Murray became dispirited, how could such an insane task ever be complete?

But suddenly, in 1881, he began to receive replies in the post from Dr W. C. Minor.

In each parcel came hundreds of definitions with information about where each word had first appeared, some going back hundreds of years.

The amount of work – the clarity and attention to detail – was astonishing.

Only a rich, cultured, learned man with a lot of time on his hands could perform this task.

Over the years Dr Minor's contributions came in their thousands.

In a preface to the dictionary, James Murray expressed his gratitude:

"Invaluable in enhancing our illustration of the literary history of individual words, phrases, and constructions have been the unflagging services of Dr W. C. Minor, which have week-by-week supplied additional quotations for the words actually preparing for press."

By 1889, James Murray and Dr Minor had been corresponding for eight years without meeting.

One day, Dr Justin Windsor, Librarian of Harvard, remarked to James Murray: **"You have given great pleasure to many Americans by speaking as you do in your preface of poor Dr Minor. This is a very painful case."**

James Murray asked what could be the problem for such a cultivated, educated man?

Dr Windsor was amazed he didn't know.

He explained that Dr Minor was a patient in Broadmoor asylum for the criminally insane.

He was an American who shot and murdered an innocent man in London, who he believed was one of a gang who came up through the floorboards at night and sexually abused him.

Dr Minor was quite insane.

It became apparent that it was his insanity that made him perfectly suited for the project.

He was cultured, educated, obsessive, fixated, with nothing but time on his hands.

Because he had a pension from the US Army and nothing to spend it on, he had fitted his cell out like a library complete with every book ever written in English.

His every waking minute was consumed with obsessive reading and notations.

The dictionary became his life.

The insane project might never have got finished without his insane contribution.

And yet if James Murray had known about Dr Minor he might have refused his help.

He might not have allowed a mad man anywhere near such a scholarly work.

In which case we might not have the *Oxford English Dictionary* today.

Which is proof of something I learned early on in my career.

In England, we are too often seduced by either posh accents or fancy job titles.

But the quality of an idea doesn't depend on the source: strategists, marketing, or creatives.

You should judge the idea on its own, not by where it came from.

A good idea doesn't care who has it.

ANY FOOL CAN MAKE IT COMPLICATED

In 1968, a young American doctor, David Nalin, was working in Bangladesh where yet another cholera outbreak was killing tens of thousands.

The main symptom of cholera was diarrhoea.

The main cause of death from diarrhoea was dehydration.

The only known treatment for dehydration was an intravenous drip, to replace lost fluids.

This was fine in urban hospitals, but most people were dying in rural villages.

They didn't have access to intravenous drips in the villages.

David Nalin had what he calls an epiphany.

Intravenous drips had been considered the only way to replace fluid without it going straight through the body and out the other end.

But what if there was another way?

He knew salt could retain fluid, the problem was the body wouldn't absorb salt.

That changed his focus.

To what could help the body absorb salt?

He found glucose would help the body absorb salt.

So now he had the beginnings of a formula: sugar helps absorb salt, salt helps absorb water.

And, in a tent in the jungle, he and a colleague, Dr Richard Cash, began to work out the proportions needed.

And through trial and error they did. The proportions were: a half a teaspoon of salt, to six teaspoons of sugar, to a litre of clean water.

In their tent in the jungle they found it worked, they began saving lives.

The proportions were right, but a teaspoon might not mean much in the villages.

They needed a language everyone understood.

So they made it simple: **a *pinch* of salt, to a *fistful* of sugar, to a jug of *boiled* water.**

Even if the villagers didn't know a teaspoon, everyone knew a pinch and a fistful.

And that formula began saving lives in remote villages.

So much so, that between 1993–94, every letter that went through the Bangladesh post office was stamped with a rhyme.

Translated into English it read: **"Good water, a pint. A fistful of sugar. A pinch of salt. End the menace for good."**

Since it was developed, it has become known as Oral Rehydration Therapy (ORT).

The Lancet said of ORT: **"Since the adoption of this inexpensive and easily applied intervention, the worldwide mortality rate for children with acute infectious diarrhoea has plummeted from 5 million to about 1.3 million deaths per year. Over fifty million lives have been saved in the past 40 years by the implementation of ORT."**

In 1987, Unicef said: **"No other single medical breakthrough of the 20th century has had the potential to prevent so many deaths over such a short period of time at so little cost."**

Journalist Jeremy Laurance said: **"Which medicine has saved more lives than any other and can be made by anyone in their kitchen, back bedroom, shantytown hut or dwelling built of sticks? The answer is: 6 teaspoons of sugar, half a teaspoon of salt, and one litre of water. Mix. Drink. It requires no specialised equipment; uses ingredients that are ubiquitous and have a long shelf life; and can be made up in any quantity – the perfect medicine."**

David Nalin's colleague, Dr Richard Cash, put it slightly differently.

He put it in terms that we could all learn from.

Something that goes against the grain for most of us in our business.

Something that many of us would feel threatened by.

But it is the secret that separates the mundane from the truly brilliant.

Dr Richard Cash said: **"It really is much harder to make something simple than it is to make it complicated."**

IN VINO VERITAS

Donald Trump had an angry exchange with the Canadian Prime Minister.

Justin Trudeau was upset with Trump for raising tariffs on imported steel goods.

Trump replied with something like, **"Well you guys burned down the White House."**

Not quite.

The White House was indeed burned down in 1814.

But Canada didn't do it, in fact Canada didn't exist as a country in 1814.

It was actually the British who burned down the White House, and the Capitol Building and most of Washington, DC.

It was in response to the US invading earlier, and burning York near Toronto.

Three weeks after burning Washington the British attacked Baltimore.

They sent a naval squadron into Chesapeake Bay, where the only thing standing in their way was Fort McHenry.

On board the British flagship, as an observer, was American poet Francis Scott Key.

He wrote the words to the American National Anthem about that battle.

Major George Armistead, in charge of Fort McHenry, refused to surrender.

So the British naval squadron unleashed everything they had, Armistead estimates between 1,500 to 1,800 shells and rockets.

All through the night, the fort was gradually turned into rubble, as Key later wrote:

"And the rockets' red glare,

The bombs bursting in air."

But in the morning, when the smoke cleared, the American flag still fluttered above the fort.

Fort McHenry hadn't surrendered, so the naval squadron turned round and sailed away.

Key was so moved he wrote the opening lines everyone knows:

"Oh say can you see, by the dawn's early light..."

And he had a patriotic and moving poem.

But to make it catch the public's imagination (in our words to make it 'go viral') he needed to turn it into something everyone could join in and sing.

He needed to put his poem to a tune.

And at that time the tune that everyone was singing, was called **"The Anacreon Song"**.

It was an English drinking song, written by John Stafford Smith around 1770.

It was the anthem of The Anacreontic Society, dedicated to the Greek philosopher who advocated the joys of love and wine.

Their main meeting place was The Crown and Anchor pub in the Strand.

Being a drinking song, it was perfect for everyone to join in all together.

Especially the rousing chorus at the end.

Which, in the original English version, was:

"And there with good fellows we'll learn to entwine

The myrtle of Venus with Bacchus's vine."

But which became, in the American version:

"O say does the star-spangled banner yet wave,

O'er the land of the free and the home of the brave?"

And that's what I like best.

You can get as fanciful and pretentious as you want in the lyrics.

But if you want it to catch on with ordinary people, you have to see what actually works with ordinary people.

And what works is music, or jokes, or stories, that you can all join in with in a pub.

Not a university debating chamber, or an art school film club.

Without that simple catchy tune, that drinking song, most of us would never have heard of Francis Scott Key's poem.

It certainly wouldn't be the national anthem of the most powerful country in the world.

BREVITY EQUALS CLARITY

These days, it seems no one can answer **'yes'** or **'no'**.

Watch any politician being interviewed on TV.

Read any advertising agency CEO being interviewed in *Campaign*.

Sit in any meeting, or read any brief.

Their entire job seems to be to take as many words as possible to say nothing.

So is it possible to give an answer in a single word?

In 1944, General McAuliffe was in charge of the 101st Airborne.

Hitler threw absolutely everything he had into one last gamble, and a massive force surrounded the 101st Airborne in the little town of Bastogne.

The 101st, being an airborne unit, was lightly armoured, the Germans had the latest 50-ton Tiger tanks.

On December 22nd, General von Lüttwitz sent in four men, under a flag of truce, to deliver an ultimatum, it read as follows:

"To the USA Commander of the encircled town of Bastogne.

The fortune of war is changing. This time the USA forces in and near Bastogne have been encircled by strong German armoured units.

More German armoured units have crossed the River Our near Ortheuville, have taken Marche and reached St. Hubert by passing through Hompre-Sibret-Tillet.

Libramont is in German hands.

There is only one possibility to save the encircled USA troops from total annihilation: that is the honourable surrender of the encircled town.

In order to think it over a term of two hours will be granted beginning with the presentation of this note.

If this proposal should be rejected one German Artillery Corps and six heavy AA Battalions are ready to annihilate the USA troops in and near Bastogne.

The order for firing will be given immediately after this two hours term.

All the serious civilian losses caused by this artillery fire would not correspond with the well-known American humanity.

The German Commander"

General McAuliffe thought it over, and sent back his reply, as follows:

"To the German Commander.

NUTS!

The American Commander"

152 words from the German commander, one word from the American commander.

McAuliffe knew that, whatever the number of words, it all came down to the same thing: surrender or fight.

So he started the fight right there in that note, forget manners, if we're going to start killing each other let's get to it.

But that single word galvanised his forces, it was just what they needed to hear.

Interestingly, McAuliffe's personal aide later said: **"General Mac was the only general I ever knew who did not use profane language."**

Because of this, the newspapers back in the USA were able to reprint it, it lifted morale by showing the no-nonsense fighting spirit of the American soldier.

The Germans never took Bastogne.

I have always found the amount of words used is inversely proportional to action.

The term 'laconic', for short, pithy speech, comes from Laconia, the region of Sparta.

Spartans were famously drawn more to action than talking.

When most of the Greek city states had submitted to Phillip II of Macedonia, he sent a message to Sparta as follows:

"If I win this war you will be slaves forever. You are advised to submit without further delay, for if I bring my army into your land, I will destroy your farms, slay your people, and raze your city."

The Spartans sent back their one word reply, as follows:

"If"

Phillip II never entered Sparta.

COMPLETE KANT

For fifty years, Sidney Morgenbesser was Professor of Philosophy at Columbia University.

So he couldn't resist turning every conversation into a philosophical discussion.

One evening he was walking up the stairs from the subway and beginning to light his pipe.

A New York cop told him to stop, there was no smoking on the subway.

Most of us would just say **"Sorry Officer"** and wait until we got above ground.

But Morgenbesser said: **"I'm not on the subway, I'm exiting the subway and practically at street level."**

Being argued with is not something New York cops take well.

The cop said: **"I told you, don't light that until you get to the sidewalk."**

Morgenbesser said: **"What harm can it do, I'm only a few steps away?"**

The cop said: **"Because if I let you do it, I'd have to let everyone do it."**

And Morgenbesser answered: **"Who do you think you are, Kant?"**

Now in one of Morgenbesser's classes, those four letters would have been heard as the name of a famous 18th century German philosopher.

But this was a cop on a New York street, and he heard those four letters very differently.

He heard them as about as clear an insult as you can get.

He put the cuffs on Morgenbesser, took him to the precinct and put him in a cell.

With his one phone call, Morgenbesser called a colleague in the philosophy department.

The colleague hurried over to explain to the arresting officer and the desk sergeant, who Immanuel Kant was, and that the remark referred to Kant's 'categorical imperative'.

Kant defines the categorical imperative like this: **"Act only in accordance with that maxim through which you can at the same time will that it becomes a universal law."**

In other words, behave as you would demand everyone behaves.

For instance, if it's okay for you to drop litter, you must believe it's okay for everyone to drop litter.

In which case, there would be litter everywhere, because that is what your behaviour implies.

But if you believe there shouldn't be litter everywhere, then you are morally compelled not to drop any litter yourself, ever.

It can't be one rule for you and one rule for everyone else.

That is Kant's categorical imperative.

So Morgenbesser's reply **"Who do you think you are, Kant?"** was a response to the cop's **"If I let you do it I'd have to let everyone do it."**

He was asking if the cop thought he was enforcing Kant's categorical imperative.

But the street, outside a subway stop, is not the best place for an esoteric philosophical discussion with a member of the NYPD.

This was Morgenbesser's mistake, he wasn't wrong, but he was inappropriate.

And that's often the problem with communication.

We don't take context into account, we speak as if we are always in the ideal setting.

We do ads that are designed to look good on the table or the wall in a boardroom, or in a D&AD Annual, or projected onto the screen at an awards show.

But we don't judge how they will work in the real world, where people are busy doing something else, on their laptop, or their iPhone, or driving or walking past.

We take a 30-second ad that was done for a TV break and run it as a pre-roll on YouTube.

We don't check where someone's head is before we start talking at them.

Which is why just 4% of advertising is remembered positively, 7% is remembered negatively, but a whopping 89% isn't noticed or remembered.

Because we're only interested in what's going on in our world.

As Bob Levenson said: **"Most people ignore advertising because advertising ignores most people."**

IMAGINE TALKING TO ORDINARY PEOPLE

The British are embarrassed to talk the way ordinary people talk, they think it's corny and patronising.

They like to flag their intelligence with long, complicated words.

But I was trained in New York, and Americans aren't embarrassed, quite the reverse.

They think it's their job to talk like ordinary people, it's more persuasive.

You might say Britain aspires to be white collar and America aspires to be blue collar.

A great example happened when Britain was at war and America was still neutral.

Most Americans wanted to stay out of the war.

The US agreed to sell Britain weapons, but that was as far as they wanted to go.

President Roosevelt was sympathetic to Britain, but he had to tread carefully.

In 1940, Churchill explained that Britain couldn't afford to buy any more weapons.

He wrote: **"The moment approaches when we shall no longer be able to pay cash for shipping and other supplies. While we will do our utmost, and shrink from no proper sacrifice to make payments across the Exchange, I believe you will agree that it would be wrong in principle and mutually disadvantageous in effect, if at the height of this struggle, Great Britain were to be divested of all saleable assets, so that after victory was won with our blood, civilisation saved, and the time gained for the United States to be fully armed against all eventualities, we should stand stripped to the bone. Such a course would not be in the moral or the economic interests of either of our countries."**

The language was typically pompous, the way politicians feel they should speak.

Roosevelt replied in similar language:

"There is absolutely no doubt in the minds of an overwhelming number of Americans that the best immediate defence of the United States is the success of Great Britain in defending itself; and that, therefore, quite aside from our historic and current interest in the survival of democracy, in the world as a whole, it is equally important from a selfish point of view of American defence, that we should do everything to help the British Empire to defend itself."

Roosevelt couldn't help by simply 'giving' Britain military aid, he had to find another way.

What he proposed was an arrangement whereby Britain could 'borrow' the weapons they needed and either return them, or pay for them, after the war.

Such a thing had never been tried before, there was no legal precedent.

It would be both complicated and contentious to present the 'Lend-Lease' bill to the US government.

So Roosevelt didn't use bombastic, pretentious, language, he spoke to human beings.

He said: **"Suppose my neighbour's house catches fire, and I have a length of garden hose. If he can take my garden hose and connect it up with his hydrant, I may help him put out his fire. Now what do I do? I don't say to him, 'Neighbour, my garden hose cost me $15; you have to pay me $15 for it.' I don't want $15 – I want my garden hose back after the fire is over. If it goes through the fire without any damage to it, he gives it back to me and thanks me very much for the use of it. But suppose it gets smashed up – holes in it during the fire; we don't have too much formality about it, but I say to him, 'I was glad to lend you that hose; I see I can't use it any more, it's all smashed up.' He says,**

'All right, I will replace it.' Now, if I get a nice new garden hose back, I am in pretty good shape."

Roosevelt spoke in what the British would call corny, patronising language.

But the Lend-Lease Act was passed by 317 votes to 17 and the US lent Britain $50 billion of military aid (equivalent to $700 billion today).

Because instead of trying to use impressive language, Roosevelt spoke like a human being.

And that's what Franklin D. Roosevelt can teach us about advertising.

That's how we should be talking to people.

Because that's what Bill Bernbach meant by: **"Simple, timeless, human truths"**.

PRINT THE MYTH

In the book *Winnie-the-Pooh*, Piglet and Pooh spot some tracks in the snow.

They decide these must belong to a Woozle.

No one's ever seen a Woozle, so they begin following the tracks.

They follow them all the way round the small wood and the tracks are joined by two more sets of tracks.

This is a surprise, there must be several Woozles.

They follow the tracks around the small wood until they're joined by more tracks.

Now Piglet and Pooh are excited.

They follow the tracks round the small wood, and they're joined by even more tracks.

Christopher Robin appears, and they breathlessly tell him the amazing news.

Christopher Robin explains to them that they have been going around in a circle, the tracks they've been following are their own.

Each time they circle the wood, their new tracks are added to the previous tracks. The Woozle doesn't actually exist.

This phenomena is known in publishing as the **'Woozle effect'**, or **'publication bias'**.

A journalist has to write up a story, they go online to look for previously published material.

They reprint what they find, assuming it's a fact.

The next journalist sees it reported by two sources and assumes of course it's fact.

The next journalist sees it reported by three sources, so it's unquestionably fact, and so on.

I've experienced it myself.

Many years ago, as a junior, I had my first interview with an advertising trade journalist.

I quoted lots of people I admired: everyone from Bill Bernbach to Buddha.

The journalist assumed that I was a Buddhist and printed it.

Soon after, another journalist read the piece and wrote that I was a Buddhist, even though we'd never even spoken.

Then other journalists repeated it and it became a fact that I was a Buddhist.

No one bothered asking me, it must be the truth because it was printed several times.

It's not a new phenomenon.

In ancient China it was known as: **'Three makes a tiger'**.

In the Warring States period (475–221 BC) Pang Cong wanted to warn the Emperor not to listen to gossip against him.

He asked him to look over the balcony at the busy street below.

He said: **"If one man said there was tiger below would you believe him?"**

The Emperor said: **"Look at how calm the people are, of course not."**

Pang Cong said: **"What if two men said there was a tiger down there?"**

The Emperor said: **"Hmmm – that might give me pause for thought."**

Pang Cong said: **"What if three men said there was a tiger below?"**

The Emperor said: **"Three men, then yes, I would definitely have to believe it."**

Pang Cong said: **"So even against the evidence of your eyes, you would believe there was a tiger if three men said so?"**

And the Emperor understood the point.

And that's how most of us think.

We don't look for facts, we look for agreement.

We don't go back to the beginning and work things out for ourselves.

We simply start with whatever the majority thinks right now, and build on that.

We don't think we follow the herd.

Which is a lemming-like way to lead our lives.

Incidentally, the myth about lemmings isn't true: Walt Disney made it up for a film.

But it's been repeated so often everyone believes it.

SAME WORDS, DIFFERENT LANGUAGE

In 1951, during the Korean War, 30,000 Chinese troops tried to take Seoul.

They attacked at the Imjin River in a 'human wave'.

This is the belief that, however many got killed, they must win by weight of numbers.

It didn't matter how many died because the Chinese had many more soldiers.

600 British soldiers from the Gloucester Regiment were defending a ridge.

In their sector, they were outnumbered 8 to 1, obviously they couldn't win.

The British Brigadier, Tony Brodie, called his superior, US General Robert H. Soule.

The American General had to decide whether to withdraw the troops.

He asked what their situation was.

The British Brigadier said **"Things are a bit sticky, sir."**

And the entire battle swung on that phrase.

The American General interpreted it to mean **"It's rough, but we can hold out."**

What the English Brigadier actually meant was **"It's bad, we can't last long."**

So the American General instructed the troops to stay put, not to withdraw.

Which is what the British did, and after four days the Chinese won.

There were many thousands of Chinese dead, with 59 British dead and 500 captured.

We lost those men because of the way that phrase was interpreted.

But how can that be when the US and UK speak the same language?

Well, because of cultural differences, the same words have different meanings.

For instance, a simple thing like the word **'aggressive'**.

In America it's a compliment, in Britain it's an insult.

The same with the word **'outspoken'**.

Americans believe plain speaking is a good thing, the British believe it's rude.

I trained in New York, so I tend to be a bit blunt by UK standards.

Jim Kelly once said **"The problem with Dave is he says exactly what he's thinking"**.

In the UK this is discourteous, a lack of manners.

Because we always need to consider the other person's feelings before we speak.

Whereas in America that would be seen as dishonest, afraid to speak the truth.

Ed McCabe describes it as like asking someone in the street for a light.

"If I say 'Excuse me, I normally wouldn't bother you, but I left my cigarette lighter at home this morning, so I wonder, if it wouldn't be too much of an inconvenience, if I could possible trouble you...' But it's too late, they're gone.

But if I say 'Got a light?' I get my light."

The main difference seems to be how we interpret respect for other people.

In the UK, respect is worrying about their feelings, in the US it's not wasting their time.

I was a copywriter in New York, and it was difficult, like learning a foreign language.

Then I came back to the UK and it was easy, everyone thought and spoke just like me.

But my American friends still struggle with UK English, they say **"Jesus, you need subtitles under them to understand what they're saying."**

In the US if you show someone a script and they say **"Interesting"** it means **"It could be good, keep going."**

In the UK it means **"I'm turning it down without hurting your feelings."**

That's why, like all communication, you should start at the receiving end.

Not with how you want to say it, but with how will it be heard.

Recently, an American friend sent me an email ending **"Good to see you're still a troublemaker, Trott."**

Luckily I can speak American and I knew he meant it as a compliment because in the UK of course that would be an insult.

That's why always we need to remember, the one who decides the meaning isn't the one speaking, it's the one listening.

The best advice I heard in this area is as follows:

"In communication it's not enough to express yourself correctly, you need to make sure you're heard correctly."

SHOPPING WARS

The Cold War was about who had most nuclear bombs: the USSR or the USA.

There were 58,336 nuclear weapons ready to be used at a moment's notice.

So it was fear of Armageddon that ended the Cold War, right?

Well no, apparently it was more to do with a visit to a supermarket.

In 1989, Boris Yeltsin was a newly elected member of the Soviet Parliament.

He was visiting America, this was something Soviet leaders didn't do.

It was a great opportunity to impress him with their technical superiority.

He met senators, congressmen, generals, businessmen, powerful and influential people.

They took him to Washington, Philadelphia, Indianapolis, Chicago, Minneapolis.

The most impressive part of the visit would be the Johnson Space Centre in Houston.

He was suitably polite about everything he saw, how similar the technology was to the Soviet Union's.

Then, on his way to the airport, they passed a small supermarket called Randall's.

He asked to stop and go inside.

They said if he wanted to see a supermarket, they'd show him a huge, modern one.

Yeltsin said no, he wanted to pick one at random, a small one that hadn't been dressed up to impress him.

So they stopped in the small town of Clear Lake, Texas, and went in.

You have to remember this was 1989, Russian supermarkets looked like badly stocked warehouses: tatty and battered boxes, half empty shelves of torn packets, badly wrapped food you had to smell first, hardly any choice, take it or leave it.

But in this little ordinary, local supermarket Yeltsin thought he'd entered Aladdin's cave.

He asked a staff member how many items they carried, she said about thirty thousand.

He started to count types of salami and lost count.

He stopped a lady who was shopping and asked her (if she didn't mind) what was her family's monthly income and how much went on food?

She said their monthly income was $3,600 and she spent around $170 a week on food, roughly 20%.

Yeltsin was amazed. In the USSR the average family would spend 60% of their income on food and it wasn't a fraction of this quality, or choice.

This hadn't been stage managed, he'd come here precisely because the Americans didn't want him to, they didn't think this was impressive enough.

Later, he would write in his book: "When I saw those shelves crammed with hundreds, thousands of cans, cartons, and goods of every possible sort, for the first time I felt quite frankly sick with despair for the Soviet people. That such a potentially super-rich country as ours had been brought to a state of such poverty. It is terrible to think of it."

On the plane back to the USSR, Yeltsin sat with his head in his hands.

His aide, Lev Sukhanov, later reported that Yeltsin said: "I think we have committed a crime against our people by making their standard of living so incomparably lower than that of the Americans."

Sukhanov said: "At that moment, the last vestiges of Bolshevism collapsed within him."

Two months later the Berlin Wall fell.

Two years after that, the entire USSR collapsed, the Cold War was over.

Boris Yeltsin became the head of the new Russian Federation.

What he'd seen in a small supermarket in a small Texas town had more impact than all the technology and weaponry.

That's the difference between something you understand and something you feel, between data and human beings.

One is much more real than the other.

TO BE OR NOT TO BE

We're all worried about criticism: what do other people think about our work?

It's normal, but that doesn't mean we should let it affect us.

For me, critics are like the crowd in the stands at a football match.

Yelling an opinion is a lot easier than actually being on the pitch.

Take Shakespeare, if he'd listened to the criticism he might have given up straight away.

Robert Greene was a famous, influential Elizabethan playwright.

In 1592, he mentioned Shakespeare in a pamphlet called *Greenes, Groats-worth of Witte*.

He wrote: **"An upstart crow, beautified with our feathers, that with his 'Tiger's heart wrapped in a Player's hide' supposes he is as well able to bombast out a blank verse as the best of you: and is, in his own conceit, the only 'shake-scene' in the country."**

Robert Greene is criticising Shakespeare, a mere actor, for daring to think he can be an author, and paraphrases a quote from one of his plays and alludes to him by name.

A few years later, in 1662, Samuel Pepys was similarly unimpressed:

"We saw *Midsummer's Night's Dream*, which I had never seen before, nor shall ever see again, for it is the most insipid ridiculous play that ever I saw in my life."

Fortunately for Shakespeare he wasn't around for the majority of the criticism.

In 1758, Diderot wrote: **"Shakespeare's fault is not the greatest into which a poet may fall. It merely indicates a deficiency of taste."**

In 1765, Voltaire wrote: **"He was a savage, who had some imagination. His pieces can please only at London and in**

Canada. It is not a good sign for the taste of a nation when that which it admires meets with favour only at home."

In 1769, Samuel Johnson wrote: "**Shakespeare never had six lines together without a fault. Perhaps you may find seven, but this does not refute my general assertion.**"

In 1814, the poet Byron wrote: "**Shakespeare's name, you may depend upon it, stands absurdly too high and will go down.**"

Even the naturalist Charles Darwin wrote: "**I have tried to read Shakespeare, and found it so intolerably dull that it nauseated me.**"

In 1907, playwright George Bernard Shaw wrote: "**There is no eminent writer whom I can despise so entirely as I despise Shakespeare when I measure my mind against his. It would positively be a relief to me to dig him up and throw stones at him.**"

In 1922, James Joyce wrote: "**Shakespeare is the happy hunting ground of all minds that have lost their balance.**"

T. S. Eliot wrote: "**We can say of Shakespeare, that never has a man turned so little knowledge to such great account.**"

And Russian author Leo Tolstoy wrote: "**For *King Lear, Romeo and Juliet, Hamlet,* and *Macbeth,* I feel an irresistible repulsion and tedium.**"

So, all great men: poets, playwrights, authors, who have criticised Shakespeare.

And yet Shakespeare is recognised as the greatest writer in the English language.

So who is right, the people who despise him, or the people who admire him?

The truth is Shakespeare wrote for the masses.

If you've been to the Globe you know the context: actors had to shout the lines from the stage, without subtlety, into an audience that was drinking and eating and shouting back.

Shakespeare wasn't writing for critics, which could be why they don't like it.

Shakespeare was writing for ordinary people.

Which is why ordinary people still use Shakespearean expressions in their daily lives.

When was the last time you heard an ordinary person quote James Joyce, or T. S. Eliot, or Voltaire, or Tolstoy?

And as for Robert Greene, who even knows who he was or what he did?

PART 5

THE POWER OF AN OPEN MIND

EFFICIENCY V EFFECTIVENESS

When I left art school, I went for a lot of interviews up and down Madison Avenue.

The new, hot, young agencies were all following Bill Bernbach's model, putting art directors and copywriters together in their own offices.

They were the agencies where all the best work was being done.

Then there were the older, bigger, agencies that had worldwide networks and massive New York offices.

They were stuck in the past, copywriters sat on one floor and art directors on another.

The copywriters sat in endless chest-high cubicles, each with an IN and OUT tray.

Traffic would drop a brief into their IN tray.

The writer would type a headline, body-copy, suggested visual, and put it in their OUT tray.

Traffic would collect it and take it to the art directors' floor (where they all sat in rows at drawing boards) and drop it into an art director's IN tray.

The first time the copywriter would see their ad was when it ran in the press.

Same for TV, the first time the writer would see their script was on the box.

The reason for this was it was the fastest, most efficient way to get ads out the door.

One floor of people talking to clients, one floor of people booking space, one floor of people writing ads, one floor of people doing layouts.

Breaking people up into separate functions meant a lot more work got done a lot faster.

And that's true, as long as the work you're doing is identical, every time.

It's not a new idea, Adam Smith had it on the first page of *The Wealth of Nations* in 1776.

"I have seen a small manufactory where ten men only were employed, and where some of them consequently performed two or three distinct operations. But though they were but indifferently accommodated with the necessary machinery, they could, when they exerted themselves, make among them about twelve pounds of pins in a day. There are in a pound upwards of 4,000 pins of a middling size. Those ten persons, therefore, could make among them upwards of 48,000 pins a day. Each person, therefore, making a tenth part of 48,000 pins, might be considered as making 4,800 pins in a day. But if they had all wrought separately and independently, they certainly could not each of them have made twenty, perhaps not one pin in a day. That is certainly not the 240th, perhaps not the 4,800th part of what they are at present capable of performing in consequence of a proper division and combination of their different operations."

So, just like pins, if you want to mass produce advertising, it's the fastest, cheapest, most efficient way to do it.

Open plan desks in open plan offices, you can fit more people in more cheaply, and crank out ads in the shortest possible time.

But what if we don't judge ads by how fast we can crank them out and how much money we can make by running a production line?

What if the client wants something that isn't identical to everyone else?

Then we may need to do more than just put bean bags, cappuccino machines, and table-football in reception.

Then we may have to start doing advertising, one at a time – not mass produced.

Starting from a point that not all problems are identical, so not all solutions will be identical, that means the process can't be identical, so we can't make ads on a production line.

Of course, there are lots of clients who don't have the time to do it properly.

The space has been booked before the creative brief has even been written.

So they do need a conveyor belt cranking out ads.

And that's okay, as long as the ads don't have to do any more than just fill up space.

As long as they don't have to achieve any sort of business result.

As long as they're being judged on efficiency, not on effectiveness.

CUSTOMER DISSERVICE

The best sniper rifle in the world is the Barrett M107.

It's a .50 calibre semi-automatic rifle, it fires a bullet twice the size and power of a normal round.

It's accurate to well over a mile.

So the world's elite forces use the Barrett M107.

In Afghanistan, a unit of US Marines got into a firefight.

Normally this wouldn't be a problem, they were equipped with a Barrett rifle.

But the Barrett kept jamming, the one thing you don't want a gun to do in a firefight.

This was now a life-or-death situation.

So a young marine did the one thing only an American would think to do.

Something that wouldn't even occur to a soldier of any other nationality in combat.

As the marine was in a firefight, he was too far from base to call for the armourer, and he didn't have any tools with him.

So he called Barrett Firearms Manufacturing in Tennessee, USA.

When the receptionist answered, he asked to be put through to customer service.

Don Cook was the person who took the call.

He asked what the problem was, he could hear the sound of a firefight in the background.

The young marine explained that his gun was jamming.

He wondered if customer service could help.

Don Cook identified the problem, the lower receiver was bent.

He was able to suggest what we would call a hack.

He told the young marine to remove the bolt carrier and use the bottom part of it to bend the lower-receiver back into position.

Then the young marine reassembled the Barrett and fired a few rounds.

When they were both satisfied it was working properly, the marine thanked him and hung up to continue the firefight.

The whole process had taken less than a minute.

Now THAT is what you call customer service.

In combat where it literally means the difference between life and death.

Only an American would think to call customer service in that situation because only in America do they have that level of customer service.

In the UK, the marine would have been put on hold because **"all our lines are busy"** while he had to listen to bad music and repeated recorded messages.

But Americans don't do that because they know customer service is good business.

In a survey, American Express found 46% of customers were willing to pay 14% more for better customer service.

Zendesk found that 40% of customers switch to another company because of a better customer service reputation.

They found 82% of customers who had switched had done so because of a bad customer service experience.

They found 55% of recommendations are made on customer service, not product or price.

Register that: doing your job well is more important than product or price.

That's a good lesson for everyone in advertising.

Because these days all anyone cares about is money.

Make as much money as we can for doing as little work as we can.

Automate everything because it's cheaper and faster.

Crank out as much as we can, as fast as we can, and charge as much as we can.

Anything to make more money.

And that may work in the short term.

Until a customer actually needs someone who can do a decent job.

EMOTION IS THE OPPOSITE OF THINKING

Daryl Davis was playing in a bar called the Silver Dollar Lounge.

Afterwards a redneck came over and said: **"I never heard a black man play the piano as good as Jerry Lee Lewis before."**

Daryl was surprised, he said: **"Well where do you think Jerry Lee Lewis learned it from?"**

The guy shrugged.

Daryl said: **"He learned it the same place I did: black blues and boogie-woogie players, guys like Little Richard and Fats Domino."**

Then they sat down and had a drink and talked about music.

The guy said: **"You know this is the first time I ever had a drink with a black man."**

Daryl laughed and said he didn't believe it.

So the guy opened up his wallet and showed him his Ku Klux Klan membership card.

He said talking to Daryl had made him reconsider his membership.

And at that point Daryl decided to connect with Klan members to convert them.

Not by fighting or by emotion, but by friendliness and simple human common sense.

Daryl said: **"That's why the best thing you can do is study up on the subject. I knew as much about the Klan, if not more, than many Klan people did. Just like any good salesman, you want a return visit and they recognised that I'd done my homework, which allowed me to come back again."**

Daryl said, every time he got someone to quit the Klan, he'd ask for their robes.

One example he gives is when he had an 'Exalted Cyclops' sitting in his car.

The man said: **"We all know black people have a gene that makes them violent."**

Daryl said: **"Wait a minute, I'm black and I've never done a carjacking or a drive-by. How do you explain that?"**

The guy said: **"Your gene is latent, it hasn't come out yet."**

Daryl said: **"Well we all know white people have a gene that makes them serial killers."**

The guy said: **"How do you figure that?"**

Daryl said: **"Well name me a black serial killer, you can't. But Charles Manson, John Wayne Gacy, Jeffrey Dahmer, Ted Bundy, they're all white, because white people have the serial killer gene."**

The guy said: **"But I never killed anyone."**

Daryl said: **"Your gene is latent, it hasn't come out yet."**

The guy said: **"That's stupid."**

Daryl said: **"Yes, it is, in fact it's just as stupid as saying black people have a violent gene."**

And the guy got very quiet and started thinking.

Five months later he gave Daryl his robes when he quit the Klan.

After thirty years of simply talking to Klan members, Daryl now has 200 Klan robes in his collection.

That's 200 people who were converted, not by emotion but by reason.

And yet, it's fashionable amongst marketing and advertising types to say that emotion works and reason doesn't.

What this misses is that we want to provoke an emotion in the recipient.

That isn't the same as making every communication emotional and ignoring reason.

Sometimes reason elicits the most emotional response.

But that seems to have escaped a lot of people.

Nigel Farage had some success in British politics, so *Campaign* interviewed him.

The amount of bile, and insults from **'communications professionals'** was overpowering.

Campaign was forced to issue an apology.

Their enquiry into Farage's success was met with a barrage of raw emotion.

Clients should ask themselves if these are the people they trust to handle their business.

I know of an old black blues musician who'd do a better job.

ANOTHER GLASS OF WINE?

Most of us have different types of wine glasses at home – why is that?

If asked, we'll probably say we need different glasses for different kinds of wine.

We might say red wine needs a wider glass for the fuller aroma, white wine needs a smaller, narrower glass for the more delicate flavour.

That's what we honestly believe about different sorts of glasses.

That the shapes have evolved over time, and people always drank different wines from the best glasses for that particular wine.

But that's not the truth – it's clever marketing.

We can learn a lot from Austrian glassmaker, Claus Riedel.

Because, unlike most marketing people, he understands the difference between talking to **'Triallists'** and talking to **'Current Users'**.

Most of us kneejerk into talking to 'Triallists' without giving it a second's thought.

We list what's good about our brand or product and look for new consumers, people who haven't tried it yet.

But what if the market has reached saturation, especially with a consumer durable: something people don't buy often?

How do you grow a market where everyone already has what you make and doesn't need any more of it?

Claus Riedel was the first person to see an opportunity in talking to that market.

Until the 1950s, most people had just one set of glasses and they used them for whatever drinks guests wanted: white wine, red wine, etc.

Claus Riedel was the first to introduce the concept of different glasses for different wines.

He said a single set won't do, you can't serve different wines from the same glasses.

So, in 1958 he launched the Burgundy Grand Cru glass at The Brussels World Fair.

It was designed to **"enhance the flavours and aromas of the Pinot Noir and Nebbiolo grape variety, specifically for Burgundy, Barolo, and Barbaresco wines"**.

A glass made specially for a particular wine was a totally new concept.

It won the Gold Medal and was acquired by the Museum of Modern Art in New York.

Then, in 1961 Riedel introduced the first full line of wine glasses created for different wines.

And, in 1973 Riedel introduced the Sommeliers Series, the world's first gourmet glasses.

Now, on Riedel's website it says: **"Claus Riedel is best known for creating grape variety-specific glassware designed to enhance types of wine based on specific properties of individual grape varieties. He was among the first glassware experts in history to recognise that the taste of wine is affected by the shape of the glass, and is credited with first discovering and developing variety-specific glassware shapes and bringing these glasses to the consumer market."**

Riedel was in charge of the family company that had been in business since 1756.

It must have been very hard to give up being a glassware company to become a specialist **'wine glass company'** especially as different wine glasses didn't even exist.

But Riedel saw it as an opportunity to stop competing with every other glassware company.

If he could make people want different wine glasses, he'd have that market to himself.

But first, he would have to build the market for different wine glasses.

He'd have to sell different types of glasses to people who thought one set was enough.

He'd have to explain why one set wasn't nearly enough.

People love to believe wine is esoteric, so the more inscrutable he could make it, the better.

Claus Riedel grew the market by adding a whole new level of complexity.

By allowing people to demonstrate being part of the cognoscenti.

He built a brand new market on the back of the glass market that existed, by reinventing wine drinking.

And that is genuine creative thinking.

YOU CAN'T NOT HAVE A BRAND

Samuel Maverick was a Texan lawyer, a politician, and a landowner.

In 1856, a neighbour settled a $1,200 debt with him by giving him 400 cattle.

Maverick wasn't interested in cattle ranching, so he kept the herd on open range land, waiting to sell it.

The convention amongst cattle ranchers was to burn their brand into their cows, to make them easily identifiable and prevent theft.

Samuel Maverick didn't want his cows branded, he didn't plan to own them that long.

But sometimes a cow would escape and, when ranchers came across one with no brand, it was assumed to be one of Maverick's.

And an unbranded cow became known as a 'maverick' for short.

Pretty soon 'maverick' was shorthand for any cow that got away from the main herd.

And eventually, any cow that was awkward or tried to escape was known as a maverick.

Over the years this transferred to humans: someone who refused to belong to a group, or conform, was said to be a maverick.

Pretty soon any free thinker, any non-conformist was called a maverick.

Originally it meant troublesome, but it became a compliment.

Nowadays 'maverick' is the name for a free thinker, a rebel.

All this began with a man who didn't want a brand and refused to have one.

So that not wanting a brand has virtually become a brand.

Because brand is just another word for image and we can't *not* have an image of something.

We have to have an image of things, that's how the mind works.

147

Image (brand) is just the way the mind differentiates things from similar things.

Take a Japanese brand called Mujirushi Ryohin, launched in 1979.

The name means **'brandless quality goods'** and their line of products was simply wrapped in plain cellophane, with plain brown labels.

The idea was to *not* have a brand because customers shouldn't pay for image.

They should only pay a fair price for the actual product.

So stamped on their plain brown label was a shortened form of their name: Muji.

The first character **'mu'** standing for 'without'.

The second character **'ji'** being a shortened form of 'jirushi' or 'brand'.

So **'Muji'** meant **'no brand'**.

The goods were plain and simple, well-designed but minimalist.

They became so popular they expanded across Japan, then the Muji concept of no brand became such a success they now have 656 stores.

In the UK, the USA, France, Italy, Germany, Sweden, Spain, Hong Kong, Singapore, China, Taiwan, Australia, India.

In New York they even sell Muji in the Museum of Modern Art shop.

They are sold at a premium up to 50% more than the marked price in Japanese yen.

So the concept of no brand has become a premium brand.

Because you can't *not* have a brand.

Anymore than you can't *not* have an image of something.

'Brand' isn't complicated, brand is simply the mind's way of differentiating one object from similar objects.

A brand is just another name for the mind's filing system.

We can't tell the public what our brand (image) is, the public don't take dictation.

The public look at our product, what it is, how it behaves.

The public then decides what the brand is based on that behaviour.

The public isn't stupid, whatever we may think.

We can decide what brand we do or don't want, but the public will decide what our brand is for themselves.

Products build brands, brands don't build products.

AIN'T I A WOMAN?

One of the most powerful rallying cries of black women's liberation was four words, repeated four times in a single speech.

It shows the power of simplicity and repetition.

Not many remember the rest of the speech, but most remember those four words.

It was a meeting on black equality and women's equality, in 1851.

The crowd was sympathetic to black male equality, but it became clear that the women the speakers were referring to were northern white women, not black southern women.

The men who were leading the meeting spoke about equality for delicate ladies who needed to be kept on a pedestal.

Then a minister objected because, although equality for men was all very well, Christ was not a woman, so women were never meant to be equal.

Also women did not have the same intellect as men and, in any case, Eve was the one who tempted Adam to sin in the first place.

None of the women present knew how to counter those arguments.

Certainly the black women dared not even speak up against a learned minister.

Eventually an elderly black lady stood up and walked to the platform.

Her name was Sojourner Truth, and she was an ex-slave.

Her speech was recorded, in her Southern slave accent, by the conference organiser, Frances Gage:

"Dat man ober dar say dat womin needs to be helped into carriages, and lifted ober ditches, and to hab de best place everywhar.

Nobody eber helps me into carriages, or ober mud-puddles, or gibs me any best place! And AIN'T I A WOMAN?

Look at me! Look at my arms! I have ploughed, and planted, and gathered into barns, and no man could head me!

And AIN'T I A WOMAN?

I could work as much and eat as much as any man, when I could get it, and bear de lash as well!

And AIN'T I A WOMAN?

I have born children, and seen mos' all sold off to slavery, and when I cried out with my mother's grief, none but Jesus heard me!

And AIN'T I A WOMAN?

Den dey talks 'bout de ting in de head: intellect is what dey call it.

What's dat got to do wid rights?

If my cup won't hold but a pint, and yourn hold a quart, wouldn't ye be mean not to let me have my little half-measure full?

Den dat minister in black dar, he say women can't have as much rights as men, 'cause Christ wan't a woman!

But whar did your Christ come from? Whar did your Christ come from?

From God and a woman! Man had nothing to do with it!

If de fust woman God ever made was strong enough to turn de world upside down all alone, dese women togedder ought to be able to turn it back, and get it right side up again!

And now dey is asking to do it, de men better let 'em."

Then she sat down and the applause was thunderous, from *all* the women present.

Because those four words said it all: **AIN'T I A WOMAN?**

They became a famous rallying cry for black women's equality.

Proving everything we need to learn about a great line.

It needs to be: simple, powerful, memorable, and capable of repetition.

And it certainly doesn't need to be grammatically correct.

WHAT WE'D LIKE V WHAT WE NEED

In 1926, Peter Freuchen was on an expedition across northern Greenland.

A blizzard blew up and he took shelter underneath his sled.

The snow built up until he was stranded inside a tiny, pitch-black space.

It froze into solid ice and was literally a snow-grave.

Freuchen tried to claw his way out but the walls were frozen hard as rock.

His beard was frozen to the sled, if he turned his head he ripped part of his face away.

The cold froze everything rock solid within seconds, there was no hope.

Which was when an incredibly creative thought struck Freuchen.

This negative might be turned into a positive.

The fact that everything froze rock-solid might be an opportunity.

What if he could find something soft and fashion it into a tool before it froze hard?

And it occurred to Freuchen that he did have something like that.

Something soft and warm he carried with him all the time.

His own faeces.

It should have been unthinkable but Freuchen had been in his snow-grave for thirty hours.

He was struck by what George Washington called **"the clarity of desperation"**.

This wasn't a time to choose his ideal preference, this was about survival.

Here's how Freuchen described the process:

"I got an idea! I had often seen a dog's dung in the sled tracks and noticed that it would freeze solid as rock. Would not that cold have the same effect on human discharge?

Repulsive as the thought was, I decided to try the experiment. I moved my bowels and from the excrement I managed to fashion a chisel-like instrument which I left to freeze... I was patient. I did not want to risk breaking my new tool by using it too soon... At last I decided to try my chisel and it worked!"

Freuchen lived by thinking the unthinkable: the clarity of desperation.

That's why I like to work with clients who are in trouble.

The job becomes very clear: it's not about what you like, it's about what you need.

The clarity of desperation.

When we were briefed on Toshiba, they'd already been advertising for five years.

Sony had 30% awareness, so Toshiba kept copying Sony and talking about the quality of their picture and technology.

But after five years of advertising they still had just 2% awareness.

Because they didn't dare to think of doing anything different to the market leader.

We told them the problem wasn't quality of picture, everyone had that.

The problem was their name, they needed to sound like a big, established brand like Sony.

They didn't want to do it but, with no choice, they ran with: HELLO TOSH, GOTTA TOSHIBA?

Did it work?

Within six weeks, awareness of Toshiba was 30%, the same as Sony.

London Docklands had been advertising for five years when we got the account.

They were still just a building site, eight square miles of mud.

The other development areas: Telford, Peterborough, and Milton Keynes were advertising themselves as great places for families to live.

So London Docklands was trying to copy them, and getting nowhere.

We told them they had to stop competing as a family destination and start competing as a business destination.

They didn't want to do it, but with no choice, they ran with: WHY MOVE TO THE MIDDLE OF NOWHERE WHEN YOU CAN MOVE TO THE MIDDLE OF LONDON.

Did it work?

Compare London Docklands today with Milton Keynes, Peterborough, and Telford, today.

The difference is the clarity of desperation.

A SOLUTION IS JUST A NEW PROBLEM

Sten Gustaf Thulin was a Swedish engineer.

He worried about the massive worldwide use of paper bags, and the effect on the planet: the amount of forests that would need to be cut down.

So he invented a bag that didn't need to cut down a single tree.

In 1959, he invented the plastic bag.

In 1962, Swedish packaging company, Celloplast, patented the design.

By 1979, 80% of Europe's shopping bags were plastic.

In 1982, two American supermarkets, Safeway and Kroger, switched to plastic bags.

By 2018, roughly ONE TRILLION plastic bags were used every year, and less than 1% were recycled.

They take a thousand years to degrade, and kill 100,000 marine animals a year.

So, not exactly saving the planet.

Quick, there's no time to think – just ban plastic bags and replace them with something natural: reusable bags.

The trouble is that people don't understand the difference between pollution and global warming.

Plastic bags clog and pollute rivers, oceans, drainage systems, and landfills.

But in 2018, a lifecycle assessment by the Danish Environmental Protection Agency found that reusable cotton bags are more harmful in terms of: climate change, ozone depletion, water use, air pollution and toxicity.

And organic cotton bags are even worse: organic cotton plants have 42% less yield and use more than double the amount of water.

Previously, in 2008, the UK Environmental Protection Agency had compared bags made of paper, plastic, cotton, and recycled polypropylene.

It found that, to do no more harm than a plastic bag, a paper bag would need to be reused seven times, a recycled polypropylene bag – 26 times, and a cotton bag – 327 times.

Senior attorney for the National Resources Defence Council, Eric Goldstein, said: "If all we do is switch from plastic to paper, we're solving one set of environmental problems and adding others."

But marketing loves a quick fix, and it's easy to appear 'woke' by giving away well-designed cotton tote bags.

So they're given away at galleries, bookstores, eyeglass boutiques, grocers, and tattoo parlours.

Speaking of marketing, the magazine *Atlantic* said: "People are depicted with their cotton tote bags at a sunny farmers' market. They wear casual, modest, warm weather clothing. They take their bags to the beach, the park, art openings, concerts, through cosmopolitan urban communities and idyllic rural escapes. They are fulfilled and creative. They are middle class. They are healthy, waste-conscious, ecologically responsible, ethnically diverse, carefree but productive, affluent, connected, tolerant, optimistic, adventurous."

In fact, the world marketing lives in.

But that isn't the world of real people, where bags are actually used for daily shopping.

In 2014, an online poll, conducted by market research firm Edelman Berland, found that half of all respondents chose not to get their beautiful cotton tote bags dirty with ordinary shopping, and chose plastic bags instead.

And it's probably even lower, with reuse rates for cotton tote bags estimated at 10%.

Because the problem exists in the world of real people.

But marketing exists in its own world.

MAKE THEM DO THE WORK FOR YOU

Steven Bradbury was a speed skater.

He represented Australia at the 2002 Winter Olympics.

Winter sports are not big in Australia, it's a hot country, so they didn't expect much.

In the 1,000-metre final, Steve Bradbury was against the fastest skaters on the planet.

The favourite was Apolo Anton Ohno (USA), then world champion Viktor Ahn (Russia), then Li Jiajun (China), and then Mathieu Turcotte (Canada).

Bradbury was the slowest and oldest person racing, so he stood no chance of winning.

But because he knew that, he had an advantage.

His coach, Ann Zhang, knew that a bronze medal would be a great result for Australia.

But she also knew that for each of the other racers, only a gold medal would do.

They were convinced they could win and would do anything to be first.

So, Zhang told Bradbury to hang back behind the leaders, let them fight it out.

All it needed was for these four hyped-up athletes to fight with one another, and for one or two to get knocked down or disqualified.

If Bradbury was simply one of the three that finished he'd get bronze.

He didn't have to beat them, he just had to let them beat each other.

And that's what he did, for the entire race he was fifteen metres behind the leaders.

Eventually it became obvious he must finish last.

But fifty metres from the finish line the Russian fell and took the American, the Canadian, and the Chinese with him.

With the all four skaters lying on the ice, Bradbury just went past them and crossed the finish line before they could get up.

And Steven Bradbury became the first athlete from the entire southern half of the planet to win a gold medal at the Winter Olympics.

Not by trying to win, but by letting everyone else lose.

THAT is a truly creative strategy.

As Napoleon said: **"Never interrupt your opponent when he is making a mistake"**.

Years ago, Avis ran their famous campaign: **"We're only no 2: We Try Harder"**.

It worked so well it began to harm morale at Hertz, the market leader.

Hertz were forced to respond with a campaign saying: **"For years, Avis has been telling you Hertz is No 1. Now we're going to tell you why"**.

It worked for Hertz employees, but for the general public it cemented Avis as an equal competitor to Hertz.

Avis had forced Hertz to do their advertising for them.

Years later, Pepsi ran **'The Pepsi Challenge'** saying 7 out of 10 cola-drinkers preferred the taste of Pepsi to Coke.

Coke were so spooked they announced they were changing their formula.

On the day they did, all Pepsi employees worldwide were given a day off.

Because Coke were doing Pepsi's advertising for them.

A few years back, the RAC ran a campaign about how they could get to a broken-down car faster than anyone else.

Rupert Howell had the AA, the market leader, as a client at that time.

He told me it was all he could do to stop the AA client from running a campaign replying to the RAC claim and disproving it.

Rupert managed to stop the AA from doing the RAC's advertising for them.

Because Rupert understood what the RAC was trying to do.

We shouldn't be frightened of provoking a response, we should be trying to provoke a response, especially from someone bigger.

If we can use our budget to provoke our opponent into spending their money answering us back, it's a very effective way of positioning ourselves in the public's mind.

By making them spend their money doing our advertising for us.

HOW TO HIT A TARGET YOU CAN'T SEE

Twenty years ago, Subaru were in trouble in America.

They were 22nd in terms of sales, way behind brands like Honda, GM, and VW.

Those brands were so massive they could advertise to everyone.

Subaru couldn't do that.

They had to choose a target where they'd get most bangs for their buck.

So they looked at their sales charts to see where they sold most cars.

The biggest market was Northampton, Massachusetts.

So that's where they decided to do their research. They targeted four main groups.

1) IT professionals, 2) outdoorsy types, 3) educators, 4) healthcare professionals.

They gave out questionnaires in the local shopping malls.

The results surprised them, nearly everyone who owned a Subaru was female, and most ticked the box as **'head of household'**.

Then, the head of the research agency said something that really shocked them.

He said: **"I'm gay, and all of the lesbians I know drive Subarus."**

Was that accurate information, or just anecdotal?

They recruited lots of Subaru owners for qualitative groups.

100% of the people who turned up were female, nearly all were lesbians.

So they decided to add a fifth group to their targets: lesbians.

Including LGBTQ publications on a media schedule wasn't new, but *targeting* lesbians was.

So they had to tread carefully.

To let lesbians know these ads were for them, but without excluding everyone else.

In other words, running ads that not everyone would get.

For instance, the headline on an ad about outdoor sports said: "GET OUT AND STAY OUT".

The headline on an ad about Subaru's obsession with quality said: "IT'S NOT A CHOICE, IT'S THE WAY WE'RE BORN".

Plus, there were clues on the cars' number plates.

XENA LVR was a reference to a lesbian icon, P TOWNIE a reference to Provincetown (a gay-friendly city), and CAMP OUT was of course a double entendre.

These ads worked so well that they decided to try mainstream media: TV.

Martina Navratilova became their spokesperson (she had won 18 Grand Slam titles and was openly gay).

Subaru had their best sales that year, ever.

But the ads weren't universally well received.

One conservative motoring magazine scornfully wrote: **"Car buyers should know that Subaru takes its role as the most pro-homosexual car company very seriously."**

Subaru received many letters from people saying they would never buy Subaru.

But they checked and none of those people had ever bought a Subaru anyway, some had even spelled the name wrongly, so they felt safe in ignoring them.

A Harvard case study later wrote that even during the 2006 recession, Subaru were the only car company not to lose market share.

Now Subaru sponsor gay pride parades, and a rainbow credit card.

They give millions to HIV/AIDS research and they were a founder sponsor of LOGO, the LGBTQ themed cable channel.

Because of their targeting, Subaru are now nicknamed Lesbaru in America.

But Subaru don't mind.

Smart targeting helped them double their brand share over ten years.

There's a line I love in the film *A River Runs Through It*:

"Talent hits a target no one else can hit. Genius hits a target no one else can see."

PART 6

IGNORANCE
WE CAN FIX.
STUPID WE CAN'T.

TOO FAR, TOO FAST

I only ever flew on Concorde once, coming back from New York.

We flew at Mach 2 which, to be honest, didn't feel any different to me.

All I knew was that the windows were too tiny to look out of, and there were no movies.

I preferred 747s.

But what did impress me was when they put the benefit into simple human language.

They explained we were flying faster than a rifle bullet.

Suddenly that was something I could understand, I couldn't even see a rifle bullet, but I was flying faster than one, that's an amazing fact.

In 1956, Tom Attridge was a test pilot.

He was flying one of the first supersonic jet fighters, the Grumman F-11.

It had four powerful 20mm cannons, and he'd been told to test fire them at top speed.

They needed to know what would happen when the force of all four guns started pushing against the plane at that speed.

How Newton's Third Law (action and reaction are equal and opposite) would affect it, what stresses it would put on the airframe?

So over the Atlantic, he picked an empty piece of ocean and fired a four second burst.

The plane shuddered but seemed okay, time to take it up to the next level.

He lowered the nose and turned on the afterburner, it came on like a kick in the pants.

He fired another long burst of the cannons, the plane shuddered again, but then the windscreen shattered and the engine started to break up.

He throttled back, he turned the plane around and put it into a shallow glide and nursed it to within sight of his airfield.

He couldn't quite make it so he crash-landed nearly a mile short, he shattered a rib and broke three vertebrae.

They investigated the plane and what they found amazed them.

It wasn't the reaction to firing the guns that damaged the F-11, it was hit by gunfire.

One cannon shell in the windshield, one in the nose-cone, and one in the engine intake.

The plane had been hit in the middle of an empty ocean, how was that possible?

Eventually they realised what had happened.

Tom Attridge had shot himself down.

It had never previously occurred to anyone that such a thing could happen, because they'd never had planes that flew as fast as bullets before.

After the first burst, Tom had put the plane into a dive and turned on the afterburner, then he fired another burst.

The plane's speed made it overtake the first burst that he'd fired, he flew straight into three of his own 20mm cannon shells.

They had the basic technology which hadn't changed in hundreds of years, guns.

They installed it into the latest technology which they hadn't learned about yet, jets.

They were so enamoured with the new technology they ignored existing basic technology.

Which is exactly what happened in our business.

The basic technology in our business is communication with people.

But suddenly we had this new technology: digital.

We were so in love with it we forgot everything else, we were blind to communication (dinosaur thinking) and people (old-fashioned).

So we ran into what we ignored, communication with people, and shot ourselves down.

Which is why, according to eMarketer, 30% of all internet users now use ad-blockers.

That's three out of every ten, and rising, mainly younger people.

In fact, to try to stop the problem, even Google has now launched its very own ad-blocker.

We're shooting ourselves down by ignoring the basics.

Like Grumman and the F-11, we'll have to learn the hard way.

MEAT V METAL

There's no doubt, the future is technology.

Technology doesn't make mistakes like us all-too-fallible humans do.

For instance, take the passwords necessary to access our computers.

Humans would pick passwords that were too easy to crack, right?

But thanks to technological guidelines, passwords are now virtually uncrackable.

Well not exactly.

The man who defined the original rules for password safety now says he got it all wrong.

That actually, all he did was make passwords easier to crack.

In 2003, Bill Burr was a manager at the National Institute of Standards and Technology.

He issued an eight-page document: **"NIST Special Publication 800-63 Appendix A"**.

It was subtitled **'Estimating Password Entropy and Strength'**.

It's the advice we've all become familiar with as the rules for creating passwords.

1. A password should include at least one capital letter.

2. A password should include at least one symbol.

3. A password should include at least one number.

4. A password should be changed every ninety days.

His advice was adopted by most academic institutions, government bodies, and large corporations.

Our password strength is automatically judged against these guidelines.

But Bill Burr now says it was totally wrong.

Because not only did these rules make passwords difficult for humans to remember.

These rules actually made passwords easier for algorithms to crack.

The Wall Street Journal had their computer security specialists check this out.

They found that a word substituting symbols and numbers (such as: Tr0ub4dor&3) would take an algorithm three days to crack.

But a random selection of easily memorable words (such as: correcthorsebatterystaple) would take an algorithm 500 years to crack.

Even though it's all written in simple, ordinary lower-case letters.

Burr's advice appeared correct because it made passwords difficult for humans to crack.

But it's easy to write a programme that substitutes the character & for 'and', or 4 for 'for', or 0 for o, or $ for s, or any number of similar combinations.

The algorithm simply runs through the alternatives.

But give it random words, without logic, and it is stumped.

Although the words are much easier for humans to remember.

What Burr had done was decide on passwords which seemed difficult for humans but were actually easy for machines.

The truth is the other way round, passwords that are easy for humans are much more difficult for machines.

This is the flaw with the human mind.

We are seduced by whatever is new and complex.

If a thing seems difficult, we think it must be intelligent.

What Burr hadn't allowed for was that humans wouldn't be cracking the passwords, machines would.

And machines can do mundane tasks many, many times faster than humans.

But what they can't do is anything unpredictable, or random, or creative.

Simply because they lack intuition.

They are incapable of creative thought, because they are machines.

Machines are very good at what machines do, but not very good at what humans do.

HUMANS ARE A NUISANCE

In World War Two, there was one big difference between allied submarines and German U-boats: the toilets.

British and American submarines had waste holding tanks, their toilets emptied into these.

German U-boats didn't have septic tanks, they emptied straight into the sea.

Emptying straight into the sea was fine while they were on the surface, but when they were submerged the water pressure meant they couldn't open the valves.

They couldn't use the toilets so they had to fill up buckets, pots and pans, whatever was available and store it all around the U-boat until they surfaced.

They could have fitted septic tanks like the Americans and British.

But they thought septic tanks were a waste of space, space for more fuel or ammunition.

So they determined to find a way to expel human waste from the U-boat straight into the ocean, while submerged.

Eventually they developed a high-pressure system able to do this.

It had two valves, one either side of a holding tank (like an airlock).

When you finished using the toilet you opened the inner valve to move the contents into the holding tank.

Then closed the inner valve, pressurised the contents, then opened the outer valve.

The greater pressure would expel the human waste into the ocean.

Because this was complicated, it needed a crewman who was trained in using it: the **'Waste Disposal Unit Manager'** (or the **'shit man'** as he was known to the crew).

On April 14th, 1945, Captain Karl-Adolf Schlitt was on the maiden voyage of the U1206.

They were submerged at 200 feet, eight miles off the coast of Scotland.

Captain Schlitt needed to use the toilet.

He wanted privacy, so he opened the inner valve himself, to move the contents to the holding tank.

But he couldn't remember the exact sequence of what came next, so he called the 'Waste Disposal Unit Manager'.

The trained crewman opened the outer valve to expel the waste, assuming Captain Schlitt had closed the inner valve.

But he hadn't, and the pressure of the water at 200 feet rushed down the pipes and straight into the submarine forcing seawater and waste to gush out everywhere.

Directly below the toilet were the submarine's main batteries.

The human waste and seawater went all over them, the mixture created lethal chlorine gas which spread all over the U-boat.

Captain Schlitt had no choice but to surface as fast as they could.

As soon as he did, British planes bombed and strafed his U-boat, killing a crewman.

The crew abandoned the sinking vessel, three drowned, 46 made it to shore and were captured.

All because the Germans wouldn't install a septic tank like the British and Americans.

Septic tanks took up too much room, they got in the way, they were for humans and humans were basically a nuisance.

Whatever the problem, technology can solve it, forget about humans.

Which is exactly where we find ourselves now.

Ordinary humans say they hate advertising, it's everywhere, it's a nuisance, it's pollution.

So the answer must be more technology and more frequent targeting.

But humans don't like the boring, repetitive content that's in the technology.

They don't want more, they want better.

Never mind that, we can solve all problems with even more technology.

Hit them faster, more accurately, more often, never mind what goes in it.

Technology is the answer, forget about humans, they're a nuisance and get in the way.

WHO'S MINDING THE STORE?

In 1972, Eastern Airlines flight 401 was flying from New York to Miami.

As they began their descent, they lowered the landing gear.

There was a thump as the gear came down, but the locking indicator didn't light up.

They were held in a holding pattern while they investigated the problem.

They put the plane on autopilot while the pilot, the co-pilot, and the flight engineer all concentrated on the indicator light.

But while they all studied the indicator, no one noticed that the plane wasn't on autopilot.

The plane was in a very slow descent, too slow to notice.

Up until the last ten seconds, when the voice recorder heard the crew spot it.

Just before the plane flew, at cruising speed, into the ground.

In 1977, United Airlines flight 2860 was flying from San Francisco to Chicago.

As they began their descent they lowered the landing gear.

Like EA flight 401, there was a thump as the gear came down, but the locking indicator didn't light up.

They were also put in a holding pattern while they investigated the problem.

Like flight 401, they put the plane on autopilot while the pilot, the co-pilot, and the flight engineer all concentrated on the indicator light.

This time the plane stayed on autopilot, but they didn't notice they were flying too low.

When they did it was too late.

They flew, at cruising speed, straight into a mountain.

In 1978, United Airlines flight 173 was flying from New York to Portland.

As they began their approach, they lowered the landing gear.

Like the other flights, there was a thump as the gear came down, but the locking indicator didn't light up.

They were also put in a holding pattern while they investigated the problem.

Like the other flights, they put the plane on autopilot while the pilot, the co-pilot, and the flight engineer all concentrated on the indicator light.

They circled for an hour trying to fix it.

But, while they had enough fuel for an hour of regular flight, they were circling with the landing gear and the flaps down, burning up much more fuel.

So, because no one looked at the fuel gauge, they ran out of fuel.

They fell out of the sky six miles from the airport runway.

The ironic thing is that those three aircraft were all found to have their landing gear locked in position, it was just the bulb that had failed.

And, in each case, everyone's attention had been on the bulb, not on flying the plane.

You would have thought someone would have concentrated on that, but no.

They assumed the plane would stay in the sky while they found the fault with the bulb.

So they ignored the most important thing because something newer distracted them.

We can learn two things from those crashes:

1. Someone should have concentrated on the big job.

2. The most recent event isn't always the most important.

Those are good lessons for us in our job.

THE POWER OF IGNORANCE

1. Someone should be concentrating on the big job: will anyone, in the world outside advertising, even notice what we're doing?

2. The most recent event isn't always the most important: like VR, or AI, or whatever gimmick is currently fashionable. It's not as important as getting a campaign, that people will notice and remember.

Where we're at now is symptomatic of how we behave.

While we write articles and sit on panels discussing the importance of the indicator light, we have a more fundamental problem that we've all forgotten about.

WHAT TIME IS THE NEXT BANDWAGON DUE?

There has been a lot of excitement among marketers about subliminal advertising.

It was the new technology, the latest thing, it would revolutionise marketing.

Except it wasn't and it didn't.

The first, and biggest, subliminal advertising craze was in 1957.

James Vicary was a market researcher in Detroit.

He conducted an experiment amongst 45,699 people at a cinema in New Jersey.

In the middle of a feature film, he had one single frame of film retouched with the words **'Drink Coca-Cola'**.

He had another single frame retouched with the words **'Eat Popcorn'**.

Film runs through a projector at 24 frames per second, so a single frame was way too fast for anyone to notice.

But James Vicary had the numbers: Coca-Cola sales were up by 18.1% in that cinema, and popcorn sales were up by 57.7%.

That's pretty impressive proof, and subliminal advertising immediately became a craze.

This being the height of the Cold War, the CIA got involved.

Their report on **'The Operational Potential of Subliminal Advertising'** resulted in it being banned in 1958.

That's how effective subliminal advertising was, except it wasn't.

Years later, a journalist, Stuart Rogers, went to check out that cinema in New Jersey.

The manager said no such test ever took place.

In a 1962 television interview, James Vicary admitted making the whole thing up.

He needed a 'gimmick' to attract clients to his market research business.

That 'gimmick' was responsible for attracting $4.5 million in fee-paying clients.

They rushed in like lemmings off a cliff.

Except they didn't, because lemmings don't actually rush off a cliff, that's also not true.

So where did that fallacy come from?

In his 1958 movie *White Wilderness*, Disney showed masses of lemmings jumping off a cliff into the sea.

Supposedly this was mass suicide because of overpopulation.

Except, again, it wasn't.

Disney fabricated the whole thing.

It was shot in Alberta, where there are no lemmings, they had to be imported.

They filmed a few dozen lemmings up close to create an illusion of scale.

Lemmings filmed on turntables to make it appear they were rushing to the sea.

Lemmings tossed into Bow River, nowhere near the Arctic Ocean.

The Alaska Department of Fish and Game were unimpressed.

Thomas McDonough, the state wildlife biologist, said: **"Disney confused dispersal with migration and embellished a kernel of truth.**

Dispersal and accidental death is a far cry from the instinctive, deliberate mass suicide depicted in *White Wilderness*."

Gordon Jarrell, an expert from the University of Alaska Fairbanks, said **"Do lemmings really kill themselves? No, the answer is unequivocal – no they don't."**

So, two things we believed simply because we didn't question what we were told.

That seems to be the pattern for marketing folks.

If there's a fad, a craze, if everyone's talking about it, we must join the herd.

Get in quick, don't be left behind.

We believe it simply because everyone else believes it.

But maybe we should learn to question things a bit more first.

Maybe we should stop rushing off non-existent cliffs after non-existent fads.

FACTS V TRUTH

In Los Angeles, in 1964, Juanita Brooks was robbed by a blonde woman with a ponytail.

The woman grabbed her handbag and a witness saw her get into a yellow car driven by a black man with a beard and moustache.

So the police were looking for an interracial couple fitting that description.

Several days later, they arrested Janet and Malcolm Collins who were a match.

Unfortunately, neither the victim nor the witness got a good enough look at the robbers' faces to positively identify them.

So the prosecution brought in an expert witness: a university mathematics professor.

The professor explained how statistics worked to the jury.

He said you can narrow down the possibility by multiplying the probability of the events together.

So he ran through the individual probabilities like this (remember this was 1964):

Probability of a woman with blonde hair: 1 in 3.

Probability of a woman with a pony tail: 1 in 10.

Probability of a black man with a moustache: 1 in 4.

Probability of a black man with a beard: 1 in 10.

Probability of a yellow car: 1 in 10.

Probability of interracial couple in a car: 1 in 1,000.

So, according to the mathematician's logic, they needed to multiply all those events together to find the probability of another couple fitting that description.

According to the data, the statistics showed there was a 1 in 12 million chance of another couple around who fitted that description.

Naturally, the jury were convinced and Janet and Malcolm Collins were found guilty.

Four years later, the Supreme Court reversed that decision.

They said the numbers may have been right, but the thinking was wrong.

This thinking has become known as **'The Prosecutor's Fallacy'**.

The Supreme Court said it was wrong to compare them to the entire population of the USA.

If they had compared them to the population of LA, there might only be three other couples that matched that description.

In which case, there would be just a 1 in 4 chance that they were guilty.

Or, more importantly, a 3 in 4 chance that they were innocent.

This is why the Supreme Court decided that maths and statistics were inadmissible as evidence in that case, and generally dubious in a court case.

Statistics and data are very easy to manipulate and what makes them particularly dangerous is they have the appearance of scientific truth.

Numbers look like facts, so data looks like reality.

But like anything, it's all in how it's presented.

In the UK, in 1995, the Committee on Safety in Medicine released a report on birth-control pills.

It said the data showed blood clots in women had risen from 1 in 7,000 to 2 in 7,000.

So a rise from 0.014% to 0.028%, nothing to worry about.

But this wouldn't sell papers, so the news media reported the same data differently.

They said the data showed the rate of blood clots had doubled.

It wasn't a lie, but it was a misleading interpretation.

In the year after the scare, unwanted pregnancies rose by around 13,000.

Because many girls and women, terrified of blood clots, stopped using the pill.

Five years later, a report in the British Medical Journal admitted the scare was unfounded.

Remember that next time you're seduced by a presentation full of numbers.

Remember that every time a media company tries to bury you in reams of data.

Data may be a fact, but it isn't the truth.

IT'S LOGIC, BUT IT'S NONSENSE

The mediaeval period is also known as the Dark Ages.

For hundreds of years religion and superstition ruled, and what held it all in place was the most thoroughly argued logic: endless debates around the seemingly logical interpretation of religion and superstition.

However ridiculous the original premise might seem, if it could be argued by superior logic it must be beyond question.

The scaffold of articulately presented logic would prove an impenetrable barrier to questioning the underlying foundation of religion and superstition.

The events that happened in the French town of Autun in 1508, illustrate this.

All living beings were subject to the law, and the law must be administered scrupulously.

It was common, for instance, for donkeys and pigs to be tried for murder, and executed.

So it was with the rats of Autun. They were accused of "Feloniously eating and wantonly destroying" the barley crop, so they must be tried according to law.

Logically, defendants had a right to be heard, so the rats were required to attend the trial.

The first problem was notifying the rats, as they were deemed to be "of no fixed abode".

So, logically, documents notifying them of the accusation and the date of the proceedings were nailed to every tree and barn, and the summons was read out from the pulpit of every church in the area.

But, despite these proclamations, on the day of the hearing the rats failed to attend.

The court was entitled to pass sentence on the rats 'in absentia', logically deciding they had forfeited their right to be heard, thereby confirming their guilt.

But the rats' legal counsel was Bartholomew Chassenee, who appealed against this.

His logical position was that every accused had the right to defend themselves, unless appearing at court put their life in danger.

He argued that, logically, the rats should be excused: "On the grounds of the length and difficulty of the journey and the serious perils which attended it, owing to the unwearied vigilance of their mortal enemies, the cats, who watched all their movements, and, with fell intent, lay in wait for them at every corner and passage."

The logical was indisputable.

So a position was logically arrived at that the rats couldn't be expected to attend the court to defend themselves, therefore the rats could not be tried.

This was the sort of scrupulous logic that was followed across mediaeval Europe for cases involving every living thing, from pigs to insects.

The fact that they were tried in a court of law, by lawyers and magistrates, gave credibility to a basically ridiculous premise.

Because we know that animals don't know what they're doing: they can't read, they can't understand the law, they can't comprehend right and wrong.

But no one can get as far as questioning that basic premise because there is too much logical scaffolding in the way.

And all the impenetrable Latin legal terminology meant simple folk couldn't question it.

Which is pretty much where we find ourselves today, with technology.

Media companies make the language difficult to understand, to convince everyone that understanding it is beyond ordinary simple folk.

Then no one can question the premise of ever-increasing technology, which is: never mind what goes in it, just look how well-targeted it is.

If we could question it, we'd see this was nonsense.

But we can't question it for the same reason mediaeval folk couldn't question executing animals — it's supported by a complex framework of seemingly impenetrable logic.

Well it may be logic, but it's still nonsense.

WHAT DO YOU WANT, BLOOD?

George Washington had been the first President of the USA.

In 1799, he woke up at 2am with an inflamed throat.

At 7.30am, Dr James Craik arrived, he'd been Washington's doctor for forty years.

He knew exactly the treatment for an inflamed throat.

It was the same as the treatment for fever, consumption, or madness.

He immediately applied leeches and drained 14oz of blood from Washington.

Two hours later the symptoms, and the pain, were worse.

Another doctor, Elisha Dick, arrived.

At 9.30am they applied more leeches and drained another 18oz of blood.

But the symptoms grew worse.

A third doctor, Gustavus Brown, arrived.

He diagnosed quinsy and severe tonsillitis, and prescribed more bleeding.

And at 11.00am more leeches were applied and another 18oz of blood drained.

But Washington's symptoms still got worse.

It needed an emergency procedure to save his life.

The very best medical minds in the country were in attendance, and they chose to use the full extent of measures known to them.

Over the next few hours they applied more and more leeches, and drained another 32oz of blood from him.

All told, since the doctors arrived, they had drained over 80oz of blood from Washington.

That's about 5 pints (2.36 litres), roughly half his body's total supply.

So the best medical minds available had extracted blood.

When it didn't work, they had doubled down on their treatment.

And when that didn't work they had doubled down again.

And as a result of their treatment, at 10pm that night, George Washington died.

After his death, Dr Craik admitted their treatment might possibly have been flawed.

He said: **"If we had taken no more blood from him, our good friend might have been alive now."**

Which is very similar to the position we find ourselves in with digital media.

Media gurus told us it was the answer to everything and the end of all other advertising.

They had their clients put a lot of money into it, but it didn't work.

So media gurus told clients to put more money into it, but it still didn't work.

And the media gurus' answer was for clients to put even more money into it.

Then, when all the money was gone and it hadn't worked, the media gurus did what George Washington's doctors did.

They admitted they might have been slightly wrong after all.

For instance, 50% of online display ads are unviewable (*The Wall Street Journal*).

The rate of engagement among brand fans on Facebook is 7 in 10,000.

One viewer in every thousand clicks on a banner ad and only 38% of web traffic is human.

Adults spend more time watching TV than all other leisure activities combined (US Bureau of Labour Statistics).

You would have thought facts like these would have made media gurus more cautious about digital media.

But like Washington's doctors, it seems they've only got one solution.

Remember the old saying: **"When the only tool you've got is a hammer every problem looks like a nail"?**

Media gurus have only got a hammer, but they think it's a Swiss army knife.

CREATIVE DISOBEDIENCE

In 1976, Niki Lauda was Formula One world champion.

So when he said the track at Nürburgring was too dangerous, he expected to be listened to.

But he wasn't.

Everyone ignored him and the race went ahead.

During the race Niki Lauda was proved right, he crashed and died.

Well almost, he was trapped in a burning car, crash helmet melting over his head and face.

He inhaled toxic burning gases deep into his lungs.

His hair, his ear, his eyelids, were scorched off and his whole head was terribly burned.

In hospital he was in a coma, and given the last rites because of his impending death.

But he didn't die, he forced himself to recover.

And bandaged all over, just six weeks later, he was in a Formula One car racing again.

He lost the world championship by a single point, to the man who'd carried on racing all the time Lauda was in the coma.

Niki Lauda learned never to trust anyone else's opinions about anything.

The next year they used skin from his remaining ear to rebuild his eyelids, he got back in a Formula One car and won the world championship again.

This time he did it in a damaged car having driven over the wreckage of another crash, ignoring what his oil-pressure light said for the last eight laps.

Seven years later, after everyone said he was finished as a driver, he came out of retirement to win the world championship for the third time, beating Alain Prost by half a point.

He learned to listen to no one but himself.

He'd also learned to fly and started his own airline, Lauda Air.

In 1991, one of Lauda Air's Boeing planes crashed outside Bangkok, killing 223 people.

Lauda demanded to know from Boeing what the cause was.

Boeing said the engine's reverse thrust had deployed in mid-air, but this was recoverable.

Lauda didn't see how a plane's engines suddenly going backward was recoverable.

Boeing insisted it was, so it must be the fault of Lauda Air not Boeing.

Lauda wouldn't accept it, he went to Boeing in Seattle and insisted they set up the flight simulator to replicate exactly what happened on the plane.

Boeing said it was a matter for them, Lauda said: **"It is my plane. My name. My damage."**

Eventually they were forced to comply.

Lauda was an experienced pilot, but in fifteen attempts on the simulator he couldn't recover the plane from sudden reverse thrust, he crashed every single time.

Lauda insisted Boeing release a statement accepting full responsibility.

Boeing's lawyers said it would take them three months to draught a response that they'd be happy with.

So did Niki Lauda complain, did he sulk, or did he just sit and wait meekly?

He did none of these, he called a press conference, he told the world's media that if Boeing was convinced it was recoverable, they should pick their two most experienced pilots.

He'd go up in a plane with them and, in mid-air, they'd reverse the thrust.

If Boeing was right they'd recover the plane, if Boeing was wrong they'd all die, in front of the world's media.

Of course Boeing couldn't do that, so they were forced to issue a statement admitting that the plane couldn't be recovered and accepting full responsibility.

Niki Lauda did that because he'd learned what happened when he trusted other people's opinions over his own.

There's a lot of pressure not to make a fuss, to keep quiet, to let the experts make the decisions.

But he'd learned, either way, we still take the consequences of what happens.

Alex Ferguson was once asked why he always ignored the press's advice.

He said: **"I'd rather be hanged for my own mistakes than for someone else's."**

THEORY V REALITY

1981 was the height of the Cold War.

It's difficult to imagine now, but there wouldn't be any negotiations, there wasn't time.

All over the world men were sitting in silos waiting to press buttons.

The instant they got the call they would each press their button.

Once it was pressed, the missiles couldn't be recalled.

That was it, thousands of missiles, each many times more destructive than Hiroshima.

And all it took to start it was for the US president to use his launch codes first.

No one knew if there would be any survivors.

No one knew if there would be anything left of the world.

That's when Roger D. Fisher made his proposal.

He was founder and director of the Harvard Negotiation Project.

He knew that the president was accompanied at all times by a young naval officer who carried a briefcase with the nuclear codes in it.

Fisher proposed that, instead of the briefcase, the nuclear codes be inserted into a capsule that was implanted into the naval officer's chest.

And, to fire the missiles, the president would have to kill the officer and cut him open to get the codes.

Fisher described his reasoning this way:

"My suggestion was quite simple: Put that needed code number in a little capsule, and then implant that capsule right next to the heart of a volunteer.

The volunteer would carry with him a big, heavy butcher knife as he accompanied the president.

If ever the President wanted to fire the nuclear weapons, the only way he could do so was for him first, with his own hands, to kill one human being.

The president says, 'George, I'm sorry but tens of millions must die.'

He has to look at someone and realise what death is – what an innocent death is.

Blood on the White House carpet. It's reality brought home."

So what was the Pentagon's reaction to Fisher's proposal?

"When I suggested this to friends in the Pentagon they said 'My God, that's terrible. Having to kill someone would distort the president's judgement.

He might never push the button.'"

The reaction of the people in the Pentagon is interesting.

They're prepared for the president to push the button that kills tens of millions of people, but they're horrified at the thought of him having to personally kill a single person.

When it's personal, they see the single killing as a more horrifying act than the impersonal killing of tens, maybe hundreds, of millions.

Because in one case, death is a reality, in the other case it's theoretical.

This is how human beings are. It's exactly how we behave in our world.

We are very confident in our pronouncements about what will or won't work out in the world, because we don't venture out into the real world.

If we need to know we have researchers do that for us.

To observe people from behind a two-way mirror.

As if our world is reality and they are merely fish in a tank, to be studied occasionally.

So we do ads that are totally detached from their world and only make sense in ours.

We don't want the grubby reality of their world polluting our award-winning art.

After all, no one we know will ever see our work in that dull, boring world. Our work gets seen in Cannes.

We don't need crude, grubby reality distorting our fine sensibilities.

PART 7

REAL IGNORANCE BEATS FALSE KNOWLEDGE

BRIEFING ON A NEED-TO-KNOW BASIS

In November 2017, officers of the 11th precinct were preparing for a drug raid.

They had information that there were two suspicious men selling drugs, in front of a house in Detroit.

They'd just been told that a lot of big, tough, armed men had gone into the house.

So the house was obviously a drug den and they needed to bust it.

So the officers were hyped-up when they saw the two men selling drugs in the street.

They approached the men.

They yelled: **"Police, you're under arrest."**

The men yelled back: **"Get the fuck outa here, you'll ruin everything."**

The police yelled: **"Get on the ground motherfuckers."**

The men yelled: **"Back the fuck off."**

One of the officers pulled out his gun, grabbed the men and slammed them to the ground.

The men yelled: **"Are you fucking crazy?"**

The officer yelled: **"Shut the fuck up."**

The men started fighting, more men rushed out of the house.

As the police were fighting with the suspects outside, more police from the 11th precinct rushed up and began fighting with the men from inside the house.

Suddenly dozens of big strong men were trading punches and yelling.

But the men inside weren't drug dealers at all, they were police from the 12th precinct.

Two dozen huge well-armed cops from the 11th and 12th precincts began beating the hell out of each other.

Inside the house, on the porch, on the path, in the street, the neighbours stood and watched with their mouths open.

They knew that the police from the 12th precinct (inside the house) were conducting a drug-sting operation to catch people buying drugs.

That's why they were in plain clothes, dressed as drug dealers.

Everyone, 12th precinct and neighbours, wondered what the hell the 11th precinct were doing, suddenly showing up and starting a fight.

Even after it became apparent that they were all cops, the fighting carried on.

The 12th precinct yelling the 11th precinct had no business conducting a sting three blocks inside their territory.

The 12th precinct also yelling the 11th precinct had no business raiding the house without a search warrant.

By the time the fighting died down, several cops had to be taken to hospital.

Guns were drawn and night-sticks were used, but luckily no one was killed.

Detroit Chief of Police, James Craig, said it was the most embarrassing incident in his 40-year career: **"Like the Keystone Cops."**

Internal Affairs investigated to find exactly what went wrong.

But it's pretty obvious what went wrong.

Neither side was talking to the other, because each side thought they were in charge.

That's what happens when one side doesn't talk to the other.

When media books the space before talking to creative.

When planning writes the brief before talking to creative.

Because they've decided they're the most important part and don't need to discuss it with anyone else.

Everyone else will just have to fit in with whatever they've decided.

No surprise it doesn't work out very well then.

When one bunch of people decide they're the ones that are important, and they don't need to discuss their part with anyone else, guess what happens.

DO THE OPPOSITE

The California Coastal Records Project was founded in 2002.

The purpose was to document the California coastline with photography.

So they flew the entire length of California in a helicopter, taking ten photographs every mile, twelve thousand pictures in all.

In 2004, the project won the Ansel Adams Award for Conservation Photography.

But not everyone was impressed.

Barbra Streisand heard one of the pictures was her beachfront home in Malibu.

So she sued them for fifty million dollars, for invasion of privacy.

On the website, her home was simply **'Image 3850'** and had been viewed four times.

But immediately news of the lawsuit became public everyone wanted to see the picture.

Soon it had been viewed over a million times.

Associated Press picked it up and it ran in publications worldwide.

Before she tried to get it removed, no one even knew about it.

Once she issued such a massive lawsuit, the picture became a must-see.

Not only that, but the judge dismissed the case and Barbra Streisand had to pay the photographer's legal fees of $155,567.

By trying to censor the picture she created the exact opposite of what she wanted.

This is now known as the **'Streisand effect'**.

People don't want to do what they're told to do, they want what they're told NOT to do.

This is an amazing discovery that advertisers still haven't caught onto.

Advertisers convince themselves that people must be told what to do.

This is because they believe people are robots.

It doesn't occur to them that people will work out for themselves what to do, thanks.

Only the best advertising treats people as if they had brains.

But, of course, examples of this are few and far between.

The first example of treating people as if they had brains was Volkswagen.

They advertised their car as: smaller, cheaper, simpler, less impressive.

Consequently VW were: economical, reliable, functional.

VW became the car for people who weren't interested in impressing other people.

Unlike Detroit, the image was the car for people who thought for themselves.

Volkswagen is now the biggest car manufacturer in the world, and Detroit is practically non-existent.

Because, unlike Detroit, VW didn't brag about their car, they did the opposite.

Avis was another example of the opposite of bragging.

They didn't advertise with pretty girls and smiling drivers in beautiful locations.

They said we aren't the biggest, we are only number two.

So why go with us?

Well we have to try harder than number one (not named, but obviously Hertz).

Number one can be complacent, we can't, we have to make sure our service is better.

Avis did the opposite of bragging.

That's why Avis was able to start battling Hertz for first place.

Apple didn't brag about how big and successful they were, they did the opposite.

In over fifty commercials, Apple didn't claim to be better than other computers.

They just had two guys, Mac and PC, chatting.

Very low-key little sitcoms, never mentioning the competition (obviously Microsoft), just using the generic term PC.

And by doing the opposite of bragging, by allowing people to use their brains, Apple is now the biggest brand in the world.

Maybe we should stop telling people what to do.

Maybe we should trust people to use their brains.

IT'S RIGHT BECAUSE EVERYONE'S DOING IT

In 1990, I was doing a recording with Adam Faith, the pop star.

Adam fancied himself as an entrepreneur and began talking about investments.

GGT had become a public company and I had money sitting in the bank.

Adam said I was nuts, you don't leave money in the bank, you put it to work.

He had all his money with an expert, I should come and meet him, all Adam's famous friends invested with him.

So, after the recording, Adam took me in his Rolls-Royce to see the expert.

He had impressive offices in the West End, he smoked a cigar and offered me a glass of champagne, he told me about his impressive list of famous clients.

The whole thing made me very uncomfortable.

It didn't feel professional, it didn't feel business-like.

So I said I'd think about it, and left it at that.

A few months later I saw in the *Evening Standard* the company had gone bankrupt and 'the expert' had been arrested.

He was £34 million in debt (around £75 million today) and looking at ten years in jail for dozens of counts of fraud.

Among the famous people who lost a fortune were: Michael Winner, Sebastian Coe, Frederick Forsyth, and Adam Faith.

People invested with him because of all the other famous people doing it.

They didn't want to be left out.

Stephen Greenspan was Professor of Psychology at the University of Colorado.

He was fascinated by what makes people gullible.

He wrote a book: **Annals of Gullibility: Why We Get Duped and How to Avoid It**.

His book was a comprehensive study on the subject of gullibility, published in 2008.

Two days after it was published he found he'd been defrauded of most of his life savings by Bernie Madoff.

Madoff ran the largest Ponzi scheme in history and his clients lost around $18 billion.

Everyone trusted him because of his famous clients, no one wanted to be left out.

Famous people who lost a fortune included: Stephen Spielberg, Kevin Bacon, John Malkovich, and Jeffrey Katzenberg.

Isaac Newton was probably the most intelligent person who ever lived.

In 1720, he invested in the South Sea Company, the hottest stock in England.

When he'd seen 100% growth in the value of his shares, he cashed them in.

He walked away with £7,000 profit (around £1.3 million today).

But everyone continued buying the stock, he didn't want to be left out.

So he used every penny he'd made to buy more shares.

When the crash came, he eventually lost £20,000 (nearly £4 million today).

As he said: **"I can calculate the motion of the heavens but not the madness of man."**

If Isaac Newton is gullible, what chance have the rest of us got?

So we shouldn't be surprised when otherwise intelligent people in our business are gullible.

If everyone else is shifting their budget online, they don't want to be left out.

Even though, as Bob Hoffman shows, 43% of mobile ad impressions are fraudulent.

Even though it's accepted that only 52% of web traffic is human.

This from a study of a billion ad impressions across a thousand mobile apps.

A further study shows that 88% of marketers confirm online advertising has no measurable impact on their business.

But despite this, everyone does it, because everyone does it.

The rational mind might fear failure, but the emotional mind fears being left out.

OLD PEOPLE V YOUNG PEOPLE

Frank and Margaret Corti were in bed trying to sleep.

It was 6.00am and they'd finally managed to doze off.

As usual the person living next door had kept them awake all night.

Frank and his wife were a quiet couple, they were both 72 years old.

Living next door was 23-year-old Gregory McCallum, who liked to drink, take drugs, play deafeningly loud music, and party all through the night.

Eventually, around 2.30am, Frank had to call the police to try to quiet him down.

Then at 6.30am McCallum started pounding on their front door.

He was still drunk and angry and he wanted revenge for them spoiling his fun.

They lay in bed and tried to ignore him, but they couldn't sleep.

Eventually, they got up, got dressed and went downstairs.

It was 8.00am and standing in their passage was McCallum with a knife and a knuckleduster.

He'd broken in, and he had a furious rage in his eyes.

He slashed at Frank Corti with the blade, a vicious swing.

McCallum was a young man in the prime of his life, Frank Corti was an old-age pensioner, even without the blade it wouldn't have been a fair fight.

And it wasn't.

Frank leaned back and avoided the knife, as he did he unleashed a right jab which caught McCallum square in the mouth.

As McCallum staggered back and dropped the knife, Frank followed through with a left hook which flattened his nose.

As McCallum was on the way down, Frank put everything behind another right which snapped his head back, closed his eye and knocked him out.

As Frank said: **"He went down like a sack of spuds."**

What McCallum hadn't known was that Frank had been a champion boxer in his youth.

As Frank said himself, you don't forget it, it just stays automatic.

Frank's wife had already called the police.

They came prepared to take the victim of a violent attack to hospital, but it wasn't the one they expected.

Frank said he had to 'restrain' McCallum, the police said **"He looked like a car-crash victim."**

His mouth was bloody and split, his nose was broken, and one eye was swollen black and shut tight.

When the case came to court, McCallum was given four years for burglary.

I think he should have been found guilty of stupidity.

He thought because Frank Corti was old he was useless.

Anyone who classes people according to a bigoted view is stupid.

Classing all old people the same is like classing all BAME people, or women, or disabled people, or LGBTQ people as the same.

Classing old people as useless stems from the days when all work was physical.

Young men were much better at physical work.

Like football: your best years are in your 20s, by the time you're 30 it's pretty much over.

But that's players, not managers.

There aren't many football managers in their 20s, because management isn't about physical ability, it's about thinking.

And that doesn't get worse as you get older, quite the reverse.

Alex Ferguson is considered one of the greatest and most successful managers, ever.

He was 72 when he retired, and he'd just won the Premier League for the 13th time.

Not because he was young or old, but because he was good.

Let's stop the fallacy that young people are better at everything and old people are past it.

Let's just judge people as individuals, it's smarter.

UBER ALLES

When Uber launched in London, in June 2012, it was a difficult time.

London had a well-developed transport system aside from trains and buses.

There were 3,000 private car hire firms.

Just one of those, Addison Lee, had 4,500 cars and turned over £90 million a year.

And the ability to order a cab over a smartphone wasn't by any means unique.

Hailo had 9,000 black cabs available on its app.

So London was a tough city to break into.

In the early days, Uber had fifty drivers doing thirty trips in 24 hours.

Their office staff consisted of three people, one of them was an intern.

The head of the London operation, Jo Bertram, tried everything to get publicity.

But the news channels just weren't interested.

Who wanted a story about another private car hire firm opening up?

But then, in 2014, something happened to change that completely.

Uber's biggest competitor put them on the map and gave them more publicity than they could dream of.

On 11 June, London's black cab drivers went on strike against Uber.

Black cabs blocked Lambeth bridge.

Black cabs blocked the roads around Whitehall, Trafalgar Square and the West End.

There was total gridlock in Westminster and Piccadilly.

Central London was brought to a standstill by 8,000 black cabs protesting against Uber.

It was on every news broadcast, on every TV station, on every radio station, in every newspaper.

For two years, Jo Bertram had tried to get an interview, no one wanted to know.

Suddenly her phone was ringing off the hook.

She did her first interview with Sky News at 6.30am, and fifteen more after that.

Uber went from being a name no one had heard of, to the hottest topic on the news.

Everyone wanted to find out why black cabs were so scared of Uber.

It came across that Uber was the future and black cabs were stuck in the past.

Cabbies didn't want people to be able to hire private cars instantly, in the street from their smartphones.

And they didn't want black cab fares undercut by a third.

The taxi strike had given Uber more airtime than they could ever have afforded, and more cachet than any advertising campaign.

Suddenly everyone wanted to use Uber, downloads of the Uber app jumped by 850%.

They seemed new, and fashionable, and smart.

Four years later there were 25,000 Uber drivers, more than black cab drivers.

And another Uber trip starts every two seconds.

They now have 100 staff in their office, and operate in fifteen cities in the UK.

All because the black cab drivers did what Uber couldn't do for themselves.

By confronting a smaller opponent they elevated that opponent, in the public's mind, up to a position of parity.

Suddenly, Uber was seen as their only serious competition.

Which is why I always advocate to clients that the very best advertising will be a campaign that the competition will try to get banned.

That should be our objective: advertising that the competition tries to get banned.

Because if the competition isn't trying to get it banned it means it isn't hurting them.

And if we aren't hurting our competitors what are we doing?

As they used to say in New York, **"If it ain't hurting, it ain't working."**

That's how you spot a great campaign.

When you can provoke the competition into doing your advertising for you.

STEP OUTSIDE YOUR MIND

Lindon Moss is a 160-acre peat bog in Wilmslow, Cheshire.

Andy Muld and Stephen Dorley were workers at the local peat-processing plant.

One day in 1981, they noticed something the size of a football amongst all the peat on the conveyor belt.

They lifted it off and started scraping the peat away.

It was a human skull, with the remains of an eye and hair still attached.

They called the police and the police knew immediately whose skull it was.

For twenty years they'd been trying to prove that Peter Reyn-Bart murdered his wife.

Malika Reyn-Bart went missing in 1960.

A year later, Peter Reyn-Bart was heard bragging in a pub that he'd murdered her and buried her.

The police dug up his garden but they couldn't find anything.

For twenty years, Reyn-Bart thought he'd got away with it.

Now, faced with the evidence of his wife's remains, he broke down and confessed.

He and his wife hadn't had sex for ages.

One day he came home and found her in bed with another man.

The man ran out, and Reyn-Bart and his wife had a terrible row.

She threatened to reveal to the police that he was a homosexual.

At that time, it was illegal and could mean public shame, arrest, even prison.

So he killed her and dismembered her body.

They lived on the edge of the peat bog, so he buried the parts in various places there.

He never expected it to be found, when it was, he confessed.

While he was awaiting trial, the police sent the skull for carbon dating.

The skull was found to be nearly two thousand years old.

It belonged to a woman who died around 210 AD, it wasn't his wife's at all.

Reyn-Bart immediately retracted his confession, but it was too late.

He was tried, found guilty and sentenced to life imprisonment.

All because he'd been living in his own reality.

His mind was so full of the crime he'd committed that it became his entire world.

He concentrated on it until other possibilities stopped existing.

And he was undone by his inability to see anything outside his own bubble.

That's what the human mind does.

We concentrate on a problem until it expands to become our whole world.

We can't escape the problem, so there's no possibility of thinking outside it.

When we find ourselves in a rut, we need someone who isn't involved to help us escape.

In the early 1960s, the owner of Levy's Rye Bread approached Bill Bernbach with a problem.

He said his packaged rye bread wasn't selling, he was desperate.

Bernbach asked him where he was advertising it.

The owner said: **"Where else? *The Jewish Chronicle* of course."**

Bernbach said: **"That's your problem, Jews won't eat packaged rye bread, they want fresh. You have to sell it to gentiles who don't know the difference."**

The owner said gentiles wouldn't eat rye bread.

But Bernbach's agency did the campaign YOU DON'T HAVE TO BE JEWISH TO LOVE LEVY'S REAL JEWISH RYE.

It ran as posters in subway stations all over New York City.

Levy's became the biggest-selling rye bread in the city, then NY state, then the USA.

Now rye bread is a staple in every delicatessen across America.

All because the owner asked someone who was outside the problem to help.

Someone whose mind wasn't consumed by the problem.

Someone who could see a world of possibilities outside the limits the mind had set.

WHEN YOU ADVERTISE THE COMPETITION

In 1938, Orson Welles broadcast *The War of the Worlds* on radio.

He broadcast it as live newsflashes across America, and everyone believed it was true.

Millions panicked and ran into the streets screaming, thousands got into their cars and headed for the hills, dozens suffered heart attacks from fear, some even jumped off buildings in sheer terror.

It was the event that made Orson Welles' reputation as a creative enfant terrible.

Before he'd only been known in New York, after he was known all across America.

Newspaper headlines like:

"RADIO LISTENERS IN PANIC TAKE WAR DRAMA AS FACT" (*New York Times*).

"U.S. TERRORISED BY RADIO MEN FROM MARS" (*San Francisco Chronicle*).

"RADIO FAKE SCARES NATION" (*Chicago Herald*).

The story is so well known it's become legend.

Well it may be legend, but it isn't true.

In actual fact, very few people heard that radio broadcast.

Those that did didn't treat it seriously.

It was broadcast on CBS radio and Frank Stanton, the President of CBS, said, **"Most people didn't hear the show, and those who did took it as a prank and accepted it that way."**

The C. E. Hooper Company phoned 5,000 households, for its national ratings survey, during the broadcast and found that less than 2% were listening.

A letter from a confused reader to the *Washington Post* said, **"During the broadcast I walked along F Street, in many stores radios were playing but I observed nothing of the supposed 'terror of the populace' because there was none."**

Ben Gross, Radio Editor of the Daily News said, **"There was no hysteria, in fact the streets were nearly deserted."**

So how did the myth that a radio programme created mass panic come about?

The truth is, it was the newspapers who built it up out of all proportion.

Radio was a relatively new medium in 1938 and, in America, radio was commercial.

For several years radio had been siphoning advertising away from print media.

The newspapers were looking for any way to discredit radio.

That's why they took advantage of Orson Welles' broadcast which used fake news.

The New York Times said, **"Radio is new but it has adult responsibilities, and it has not yet mastered itself nor the material it uses: interweaving blood-curdling fiction with news flashes offered in exactly the same way that real news would have been given."**

Editor & Publisher wrote, **"The nation as a whole continues to face the danger of incomplete, misunderstood news over a medium which has yet to prove it is competent to perform the job."**

So, newspapers attempted to make radio unattractive to advertisers by discrediting it.

But they did the opposite.

Advertisers began to believe in the power of radio, they'd never known newspapers to provoke such a response.

Immediately after the stories ran, The Campbell Soup Company struck a deal with Orson Welles to sponsor his Mercury Theatre of the Air, and they changed the name to The Campbell Playhouse.

The press notoriety helped Orson Welles walk into a job as a director in Hollywood.

He had such a reputation he was given carte blanche to write a script, cast, light, edit, direct, and act in his first film, however he saw fit.

Something unheard of, but he was allowed due to the reputation the papers gave him.

That film was *Citizen Kane*, usually voted the best film of all time by cinema experts.

And none of it might have happened if the newspapers hadn't tried to kill off radio.

LEGENDS IN OUR OWN LUNCHTIME

Each episode of *The Simpsons* takes nine months to make.

From idea, to writing, to recording, to animation. No wonder they cost a fortune.

With celebrity voice-overs and no expense spared, it's no surprise *The Simpsons* is the second longest-running show on American TV.

But if it's only the second longest-running show, how expensive must the first longest-running show be?

Well strangely enough not expensive at all, in fact it hardly costs anything.

It's cheap, and quick, and easy to make: no idea, no writing, no celebrity voice-overs.

The longest-running show is called *COPS*.

All it is, is a hand-held camera following the police as they respond to real-life crime, and the results are edited down to make a TV show.

It's a very simple format, so who was responsible for such a great idea?

Well strangely enough, it was the very people the show doesn't need: writers.

What happened was, in 1989 all the writers went on strike.

So no new scripts could get written, no new programmes could get made, nothing.

Fox TV had recently launched, and Stephen Chao was in charge of finding new programmes just at the time when no programmes could be written.

He mentioned his dilemma to John Langley who said **"Take a look at this."**

And he showed him footage he'd obtained of a police drug-bust.

Smashing in doors guns drawn, screaming and yelling, shoving drug addicts to the floor, handcuffing them amidst crack cocaine and filth.

It was so riveting it didn't need any presenters or voice-overs.

As they watched it they both thought the same thing: who needs writers?

And a new genre of television was born: TV that didn't need the people who were on strike.

John Langley started by recruiting sheriff Nick Navarro of Broward County.

Navarro was up for re-election and saw the shows as TV commercials for himself.

The reviews in the papers were terrific, one read:

"We've had male cops: *Starsky & Hutch*. We've had female cops: *Cagney & Lacey*. We've had rogue cops: *Serpico*. We've had rumpled cops: *Columbo*. We've had dapper cops: *Miami Vice*. We've had dour cops: *Hawaii Five-0*. We've had everything except real cops, until *COPS*."

All over America police departments began inviting the show to film them at work.

LA Police Chief Willie Williams said: **"It makes sense for the department to receive some positive coverage and for people to understand the real-life problems police officers have to deal with every single day."**

It became a way to boost morale amongst officers, to gain respect from the community, and to increase recruitment.

By going on strike, the writers created the very thing they had tried to strangle: new TV shows.

The lack of scripts had created a new genre of TV shows.

Because someone had been creative and spotted an opportunity in the problem.

Now there are real-life shows featuring police forces all over the world.

As well as shows like: *Ice Road Truckers, Outback Truckers*, shows about emergency rescue, hospital A&E Departments, airport smuggling, even shops like Harrods.

All the writers did by striking was force people to get creative.

And people found they didn't need writers, real life was more exciting.

The TV scriptwriters had lost touch with reality, they thought they were more important.

I think we've done that in our business.

But we aren't important, the real world is more exciting.

And if we forget that, the real world will find it doesn't need us either.

MACHINES CAN REPLACE CREATIVITY

In 1891, Herbert Henry Dow invented the Dow process.

This was a method of using electrolysis to extract bromine more cheaply.

In those days, bromine was big business.

It was used in: medicines, disinfectant, dyes, photographic film, fertiliser, water-purification, fire-retardant, and pesticides.

A German government-controlled cartel, Bromkonvention, had a monopoly on the sale and production of bromine.

But Dow's new process allowed him to extract and sell bromine for less.

The cartel was selling it for 49 cents per pound.

Dow began selling it at 36 cents per pound.

The cartel warned him to stop, but he continued.

So, in 1904, the cartel began 'dumping' bromine in the USA.

This is a practice whereby the largest producer sells the product below cost, to take all the smaller competitor's customers.

Being the largest, they can afford to do this but the smaller competitor can't.

The cartel began selling bromine at just 15 cents a pound in America.

Sales were huge, but something strange began happening.

Their own sales in Europe began to fall.

Someone was selling bromine more cheaply at home.

Bromkonvention were selling more than they thought possible in America.

But their sales were down in Europe because someone was undercutting them on price.

It took them a long time, but finally they twigged what was happening.

Dow couldn't match their low price in the USA, but he didn't need to.

He just bought up every pound of bromine they were selling at the below-cost price and shipped it back to Europe.

Where he relabelled it and undercut the price the cartel was selling bromine at.

Because they were still selling at 49 cents a pound in Europe, but selling at 15 cents a pound in America.

Dow would simply buy everything at 15 cents a pound, then export it back to Europe where he would sell it at 27 cents a pound.

Of course, everyone bought bromine at the cheaper price.

The cartel was losing 24 cents on every pound while Dow was making 12 cents on every pound.

And the cartel was effectively financing him.

Eventually the cartel gave in, and Dow was free to carry on selling his bromine in America at his original price of 36 cents a pound.

He had used their own tactics against them.

While they were 'dumping' bromine in America, he took hundreds of thousands of pounds of their bromine back to Europe and began 'dumping' it there.

Dow set up the game so that either way, whatever move they made, he won.

Today, the company Herbert Henry Dow started is the second largest chemical manufacturing company in the world.

It has 54,000 employees in 160 countries and annual sales of $57 billion.

That's real creativity, refusing to be bound by the same conventions as everyone else.

Not being intimidated by accepted wisdom, however established.

That is the sort of creativity we don't see much in our business anymore.

Now we see a standard brief for a standard solution for a standard piece of content in a standard media space.

No wonder we think AI will end up doing our job.

We don't seem capable of any creative thinking.

OVER-COMPENSATE

When I graduated art school, I wanted to work on a tramp steamer.

After four years in college I liked the idea of manual labour while seeing the world.

So I went to the Brooklyn docks and signed on to a Danish freighter.

I was only a deckhand, but in the Gulf of Mexico they asked me to steer the ship.

This is done from a big wheel in the centre of the bridge.

The ship weighed 10,000 tons and was travelling at sixteen knots (about 20 mph).

They told me to concentrate on the vertical crane in front of the bridge.

Turn the wheel towards the direction I wanted to go.

As soon as I saw the crane begin to move that way, start turning the wheel back.

Don't wait for the ship to get to the setting I wanted, by that time it would be too late, the ship would just carry on turning straight past it.

It isn't like a car where you turn the wheel and the car immediately turns.

Everything on a big ship happens with a time lag.

You turn the wheel and it takes ten seconds for the rudder to even respond.

You've got 10,000 tons of water moving past at 20 mph, trying to stop the rudder moving, so you need a massively powerful servo-mechanism to turn it.

Once the rudder's moved, it needs to bite into the water, that takes another ten seconds.

When it bites, 10,000 tons of ship begins to gradually turn.

That's when you have to start turning the whole thing back the other way, twenty seconds before the ship gets pointed in the direction you wanted.

The whole process is like a huge factory skidding across the ocean.

Steer... then correct... then correct again... and (hopefully) one final correction.

To a landlubber (like me) it felt like constantly over-correcting, there was no accuracy, just big wallowing movements.

Every movement was bigger and slower than you intended, every movement was large and crude, the ship acted like it couldn't care less.

Which, coincidentally, I later found was exactly the way the general public responds to advertising.

Just like a massive ship, the public ploughs on through their life, they couldn't care less what we're doing.

If we want to get them to pay any attention at all, we have to over-compensate, we have to do much more than we think necessary.

We turn the wheel that will turn the rudder that will turn the ship, and it will always take more than we think we need.

Because, just like the ocean, the public doesn't give a shit what we're up to.

Just like a ship, we need a sledgehammer not a rapier. Rapiers are for awards juries: little clever ads for people whose lives revolve around advertising.

People who inspect advertising under a magnifying glass.

Paul Arden once told me the most important thing he learned from Charles Saatchi was: **"Think bigger. However big you're thinking, it isn't big enough, think bigger."**

Later on, I read Damien Hirst saying the most important thing he learned from Charles Saatchi was: **"Think big, if you're not embarrassed by it you're not thinking big enough."**

That's how he trained two of the boldest creative thinkers of our time.

Always assume that whatever we do, no one is going to notice it.

It has to be more shocking, more outrageous, much bigger to even begin to make a dent in the real world.

The real world where, unlike the jeweller's eyepiece that is Cannes, no one gives a shit about advertising.

PART 8

THE TRAP OF
THINKING WE KNOW

THE PARALYSIS OF THINKING

Around 2,500 years ago, Thucydides predicted Brexit.

He wasn't writing about Brexit of course, he was writing about the Peloponnesian wars.

But see if this sounds familiar:

"In general, the men of lower intelligence won out.

Afraid of their own shortcomings and of the intelligence of their opponents, so that they would not lose out in reasoned argument or be taken by surprise by their quick-witted opponents, they boldly moved into action.

Their enemies, on the contrary, contemptuous and confident in their ability to anticipate, thought there was no need to take by action what they could win by their brains."

To update that, compare it with what journalist Matt Chorley wrote about Brexit:

"Once again while the Remainers spent a lot of time talking to each other, not ruling anything out, keeping options on the table, forming groupings, having meetings, plotting plans and planning plots, they've been totally wrong-footed by more decisive opponents."

So basically, in 2,500 years we've learned nothing.

We still value process above results, we still value form above function.

Or, as Rory Sutherland says: **"The overeducated technocratic elite would rather be precisely wrong than vaguely right."**

Why is this?

In his book *The Stupidity Paradox*, Mats Alvesson puts it like this:

"For over a decade we studied hundreds of people in dozens of organisations.

We were constantly struck by how these organisations, which employ so many people with high IQs and impressive qualifications, could do so many stupid things."

Here are some of the examples he gives:

"Executives who are more interested in impressive PowerPoint shows than genuinely useful analysis.

Technology firms more interested in keeping a positive tone than solving problems.

Marketing executives obsessed with branding over any innovative thinking.

Corporations investing millions in 'change exercises' and when they fail doing exactly the same thing again and again.

Senior military personnel more interested in rebranding exercises than military exercises."

It seems what all these people have in common is the paralysis of thinking.

At GGT, we began the first real agency-wide traffic system.

It happened after we won a pitch and were given six months to produce a campaign.

Creative didn't even get briefed until the planners and client had spent five months thinking and talking about the brief.

Then creative got the time that was left, and when we presented the campaign it was rejected because the brief was wrong.

So they wasted five months (that we could have spent thinking up different campaigns) coming up with the wrong brief.

After that, we had a traffic system where every department performed to a deadline.

One of the UK's most successful entrepreneurs, Peter Wood, once told me his motto: **"Do it, then fix it."**

Don't wait to get it perfect before you start, it'll never be perfect so you're wasting time.

Legendary football manager Bill Shankly once asked a young striker why he'd hesitated and lost the ball in front of the opposition's goal.

The youngster said: **"I couldn't decide whether to lob the keeper, nutmeg him, or send him the wrong way."**

Shankly said: **"Look son, if you ever find yourself in front of goal with the ball at your feet and you don't know what to do, just stick it in the net and we'll discuss all your options afterwards."**

Or as George S. Patton said: **"A good plan executed today is better than a great plan tomorrow."**

CURE FOR DEPRESSION

IBM's president, Thomas Watson, was a dynamic man and revolutionised the company.

His motto, for every single employee, was **"THINK"**.

Which became very relevant in 1929, when the stock market crashed.

It was the most devastating stock market crash in history and signalled the start of the worldwide Great Depression.

Half the banks in America failed, unemployment was 20%, and industrial production dropped by 50%.

Most businesses were laying off workers, it was the sensible thing to do.

But Watson called his top executives into the boardroom, he said:

"Gentlemen, some of our people have had to give a lot of thought to their finances, which has distracted their attention from the main issue, which is, of course, building IBM and making it a bigger and better business.

I have not done anything in the interests of IBM for the last three weeks, I have not talked with any of you about sales, money collections, etcetera.

Because I have been running a stockbroker's office for the last three weeks."

Watson was saying that they were all paralysed because all they were worrying about was the plummeting share price and their savings.

He knew worrying wouldn't solve anything, they needed to act.

So Watson did the opposite of what every other company was doing.

He didn't lay anyone off, he kept all the factories open, producing IBM machines.

And he did something no one had done before, he took 6% of revenue ($1 million then, $18 billion today) to build the first corporate research laboratory, and put all the inventors and engineers in the same building.

It looked crazy, inventory stockpiled and the share price plummeted.

But, unlike everyone else, Watson knew the Depression couldn't last, and he wanted IBM to be better placed than anyone else when it finally ended.

Then, in 1933, Franklin Roosevelt was elected US president.

Under his **New Deal** he passed the Social Security Act: employers would have to make deductions from every worker's wages so that the elderly, unemployed, disabled, and widows with children would get financial assistance.

Suddenly, every employer needed to keep track of the wages and hours of every single worker in the country, and so did the government.

Suddenly, every company needed lots of tabulating and calculating machines, now.

And there was only one company in full production on those machines, and with a massive inventory, ready to supply straightaway: IBM.

For Woolworth's alone the cost was $250,000 a year ($4.5 billion today).

From 1935 to 1939, IBM revenue increased by 81% and continued to climb for 45 years.

IBM didn't just dominate the market, they owned it.

During that period, they invented the floppy disk, the barcode, the hard drive, the ATM.

Today, IBM employs 350,000 people worldwide, and IBM employees have won five Nobel Prizes.

All because, in 1929, Thomas Watson followed his own dictum: **"THINK"**.

As he said, himself, at the depths of the Depression: **"When is industrial progress going to start again? I say it never stopped. You are going to find that inventive genius, progressive ideas,** progressive people, have been more active than ever. Industrial progress never stops."

Or, as Bill Bernbach would later say: **"It may well be that creativity is the last legal unfair advantage we are allowed to take over the competition."**

TEXAS SHARPSHOOTER ADVERTISING

In 1894, London had 11,000 horse-drawn Hansom cabs and thousands of omnibuses.

Each omnibus needed 12 horses a day, so that made around 50,000 horses on London's streets.

And that was just for transport, there were also tens of thousands of horses and carts delivering beer, fruit, veg, milk bread, furniture, and everything else.

Each horse produced 15–30 pounds of dung a day, plus at least a quart of urine, all filling up London's streets.

You can see why, in 1894, *The Times* predicted: **"In fifty years, every street in London will be buried under nine feet of manure."**

Because the car hadn't been invented yet, and the future must be an extension of the present, so we can only predict what will happen based on what we know.

This is known as **The Texas Sharpshooter Fallacy**.

It's based on the Texan who wants to be known as a crack shot with a gun.

He gets out both pistols and begins blasting away at the side of his barn.

The bullets go everywhere, but some of the holes are naturally clustered together.

So he gets a paintbrush and paints a target around the cluster, which makes him look like a pretty good shot, it looks like he hit the target quite a few times.

We do this a lot, seeking patterns is a natural function of the mind.

We make the facts fit the thinking, which is the way conspiracy theories work.

You can see this in any conspiracy theory.

The Kennedy assassination: fuzzy, blurry photos are interpreted as snipers behind a fence. The 9/11 attacks: puffs of dust are interpreted as pre-placed demolition charges.

Paul McCartney is dead, because he had no shoes on in the Abbey Road cover photo.

One of the most enduring examples of the Texas Sharpshooter fallacy is Nostradamus.

Written 500 years ago, his inscrutable verse has been interpreted over the years.

He is believed to have predicted many events throughout history, for instance:

"Beasts wild with hunger shall cross the rivers:

Most of the fighting shall be done by Hister,

It shall result in the great one being dragged in an iron cage,

While the Rhine child of Germany will observe."

It's pretty obvious that he must be referring to World War Two.

"Hister" must mean Hitler, especially as he talks of **"the Rhine Child of Germany"**.

Well yes it looks like that, interpreted from our time.

But that's drawing a target round the bullet holes, making his verse fit our knowledge.

Because, in fact, in Nostradamus's time "Hister" was the name of the river Danube.

One of the rivers he refers to in the previous line.

But our minds simply override that and relate everything to our current experience.

Which is where we mistake subjectivity for objectivity.

We assume what we are thinking is the only way to interpret the facts.

We don't investigate facts, we start with an end point and draw our assumptions around it.

Whether that's research results: we listen for the responses that confirm our opinions.

Or media choices: we want online to work so we quote vanity metrics: 'likes' and 'shares'.

Or, against all evidence, we believe we must have an influencer-advertising strategy.

An Instagram strategy, a Facebook strategy, a Twitter strategy, a strategy for every single form of new media, we must have it simply because we must have it.

Whatever we want, we only interpret the data that fits our preference.

We must make the facts fit the conclusion we want.

So we paint a target around the bullet holes.

That's a lot easier than actually using our brains to hit the target.

YOU ONLY THINK YOU KNOW

In 1959, John Griffin was a journalist in New Orleans.

After the war, the world was changing and people were treated as equals, everywhere.

At least, everywhere except the southern states of America.

Many southerners still felt that blacks could never be considered equal with whites.

As a journalist, this fascinated Griffin.

When blacks complained, he'd say: "I know how you feel."

They'd shake their head and say: "I don't think so."

And Griffin thought: they're right – I can't know how they feel, because I'm not black.

Then he thought: if I become black I'll know what it feels like, instead of just observing it.

So that's what he did, his experiences became a book called *Black Like Me*.

First, he got a doctor to advise him on the pills to take to darken his skin, he sat for ages under a sunlamp, he stained his skin, he shaved his head, he wore dark glasses, and when he looked in the mirror he didn't recognise himself.

Neither did anyone else in New Orleans, he'd become a black man.

Then he travelled to the worst places for racism in the south: Mississippi and Alabama.

He said: "Previously, I assumed negroes led essentially the same kind of life whites know, with certain inconveniences caused by discrimination and prejudice."

But his experience shifted immediately: "Everything is different. Everything changes. As soon as I go into areas where I had contact with white people, I realised that I was no longer regarded as a human individual, I am not speaking here only of myself. This is the mind-twisting experience of every black person I know."

'Civilised' whites didn't want blacks mixing with them.

When he bought an ice cream, there was a sign in the shop clearly indicating 'Rest Room'.

He asked the man he'd just bought the ice cream from, if there was a rest room.

The man said: "You go on up that road to the bridge, cut down the road to the left, follow that road to a gas station, there's one there."

Griffin asked how far it was, the man said about 14 blocks.

Griffin asked if there wasn't one closer he could use, the man said he didn't know of any.

Later, he bought a Greyhound bus ticket and turned to sit in the large, empty waiting room.

The woman who sold him the ticket glowered at him, she flicked her head to the left.

Griffin walked outside and found a tiny, cramped waiting room full of black people.

On the bus, a white woman would not sit in the empty seat next to him.

He was made to get up and sit next to another black person so she could sit down.

He said, as a white person he'd got used to being able to walk anywhere without thinking.

As a black person, he had to plan every trip, to make sure there was somewhere he could eat, or drink, or use the restroom.

Griffin said, by being black, he learned what a white man could never learn by observing: "Blackness is not a colour but a lived experience."

What Griffin did is a great lesson for us.

Our audience is always people who aren't like us.

We think we know what other people want simply by observing them.

Then we interpret them from our point of view.

But to really know what's going on with them we must connect at a deeper level.

What Bernbach calls: "Simple, timeless, human truths."

Or as John Griffin said, when writing his book: "If I could take on the skin of a black man, live whatever might happen and then share that experience with others, perhaps at the level of shared human experience, we might come to some understanding that was not possible at the level of pure reason."

THE BRIEF IS THE 'WHAT' NOT THE 'HOW'

In 1945, the German submarine, U-864, was to take a secret cargo to Japan.

Sixty-five tons of mercury, plus the blueprints to build a jet plane (way ahead of anything the Allies had), plus German jet engineers, as well as Japanese torpedo and fuel experts.

It was a very large U-boat armed with 22 torpedoes.

A British submarine, HMS Venturer, commanded by 25-year-old Jamie Launders, was sent to intercept it.

They found it near Norway, where they expected, but they only saw its periscope, it stayed submerged, so they stayed submerged.

As both subs were under water, and so invisible to each other, it would have made sense to use ASDIC (the British version of Sonar). But Launders thought the loud 'ping' would give them away, so he used sound location instead.

For 45 minutes they sat silently. Eventually the U-boat started to move.

The U-boat followed a zig-zag course, and for three hours Launders followed underwater.

Eventually he knew he must attack, but he knew it would take a torpedo four minutes to reach the U-boat.

That meant they'd hear it coming and take evasive action.

At that time, attacks were in two dimensions: distance to target and horizontal movement.

This would be the first ever three-dimensional attack: it included depth.

This involved getting the current position of the U-boat right, but more importantly its position in four minutes' time, after it heard the torpedo coming.

Launders calculated according to speed, turning and diving ability, and what he thought the U-boat commander would do.

He fired four torpedoes at 17-second intervals: one at the U-boat, one below it, then one to the lower left and one to the lower right.

After 16 minutes they heard a massive underwater explosion.

As Launders had predicted, the first torpedo made the U-boat dive, straight into the path of the second torpedo, which made the U-boat veer left, straight into the path of the third torpedo which made it veer right.

Straight into the path of the fourth torpedo which hit it.

It was the only time, before or since, that one submarine had engaged and sunk another submarine while both were underwater.

It wasn't something that could ever be expected or taught.

So it wasn't written on the brief, the brief just said to go where the U-boat was going to be and that the job was to sink it.

The brief was WHAT to do, not HOW to do it.

Too often nowadays the people who write the brief think it's their job to write a fully detailed and proscriptive list of HOW the job must be done.

So you have people who aren't trained to do the job, tying the hands of the people who should be doing the job.

Of course, the people who write the brief should be concerned with the business problem: WHAT is the job to be done?

Those actually doing the job should be concerned only with HOW it should be done.

It's the job of the people who write the brief to get the RIGHT answer. It's the job of the people who do the work to get that answer noticed and remembered.

That's their job, that's what they should have been trained for.

People writing briefs have been trained in marketing NOT communication.

People who do the work have been trained in communication NOT marketing.

It works better when everyone does their job and lets other specialists do theirs.

IF THE HAT FITS, WEAR IT

The normal picture we have of America in the 1800s is cowboys wearing Stetson hats, driving herds of cattle.

Lawmen wearing Stetson hats in shootouts with bank robbers.

Settlers wearing Stetson hats circling their wagons against the Indians.

And some of that is true, but the part about the Stetson hats isn't.

You see the Stetson hat didn't even exist until nearly the end of the nineteenth century.

Before that, people just grabbed whatever hat was around and, one that wouldn't matter if it got dirty and torn.

So cattle workers would wear old peaked caps, or sombreros, or hats made from animal skins, or battered straw boaters, or homburgs, or pork pie hats, or derby (bowler) hats, the same hats as people everywhere.

Which is what John B. Stetson did when he was panning for gold in Colorado.

That's when he noticed none of these hats were really suited to the work outdoors.

The searing hot sun, or the icy rain, none of them gave much protection.

So he started from scratch and made a head-covering from the dried skin of some beavers.

He didn't care what it looked like, just how well it did the job.

So he gave it a big wide brim to keep the sun and rain off.

He made it taller inside than head height, so the trapped air would act as insulation.

When he first wore it, everyone laughed.

But one of the workers tried it, and liked it so much he paid Stetson five dollars for it.

Pretty soon more workers tried it and decided they wanted hats like that, too.

So Stetson made and sold a few more hats, then a few more.

And pretty soon he realised he was making more money from hats than panning for gold.

So he went back to Philadelphia and began manufacturing these unusual hats.

He called his design **'The Boss of the Plains'**.

He sent sample hats to merchants throughout the Southwest asking them for a minimum order of a dozen hats.

It was an immediate success, and within a year he set up a factory.

The name 'Stetson: Boss of the Plains' got shortened to Stetson, and an entirely new style of hat was created.

By the turn of the century, Stetson was making 3.5 million hats a year.

Around that time, they began making moving pictures in Hollywood.

The equipment and techniques were crude, they needed simple stories and simple images.

Cowboy stories were simple (good guys v bad guys) and cowboys could easily be shown by putting them all in big, distinctive Stetson hats.

By the beginning of the twentieth century, the Stetson was adopted by Hollywood as the symbol of the Wild West, shorthand for a cowboy.

And from that time, the image was born that all cowboys wore Stetson hats.

So the history that exists is not the fact, but the image.

And today, every film star cowboy, and every superstar country singer, must wear a Stetson for credibility.

Every foreign politician visiting America must be given an authentic Stetson as a treasured symbol of America's tough self-made past.

The lesson for us is that reality is irrelevant.

What the mind believes is reality, becomes reality.

So our job is to create reality, which means our media is the mind.

When Roosevelt asked Churchill how he thought history would remember them, Churchill said: **"History will be kind to us, because I will write the history."**

And he did, and it was.

A GOOD AD IS A SOLD AD

Can you make a product too well?

Can you give your customers too much value for their money?

Apparently you can, you can make a product so well it's bad for business.

When light bulbs were first mass produced, they lasted up to 2,500 hours.

This was good for initial sales, but obviously bad for repeat sales.

In 1922, for instance, Osram sold 63 million light bulbs in Germany.

But the light bulbs lasted so well that next year they only sold 28 million.

Building a better product was plainly bad for business.

Something had to be done.

They contacted the other manufacturers and found they had the same problem.

Everyone's sales were down because their bulbs lasted too long.

Making a better product was killing their business.

So in 1924, the Phoebus Cartel was formed.

It comprised: Osram from Germany, Philips from Holland, General Electric from Britain, Compagnie de Lampes from France, Tokyo Electric from Japan, and Tungsram from Hungary.

The document that was signed by all parties was headed **"Convention for the Development and Progress of the International Incandescent Electric Lamp Industry"**.

Together they decided to increase demand by shortening the life of their light bulbs.

So in 1925, they reduced the maximum life from 2,500 to 1,000 hours.

In order to make sure everyone complied, samples were regularly tested at a centralised laboratory in Switzerland.

Manufacturers whose bulbs lasted longer than 1,000 hours were fined.

And manufacturers who sold more than their allotted quota were also fined.

This led to problems.

Tokyo Electric, for instance, had seen sales rise fivefold since reducing the life of their bulbs.

They didn't know whether to pay the fines or reduce production.

But cartel members were rigorous about shortening bulb life to create repeat purchase.

In a letter to an executive at International General Electric, Anton Philips, head of Philips, wrote the following.

"After the very strenuous efforts we made to emerge from a period of long life lamps, it is of the greatest importance that we do not sink back into the same mire by supplying lamps that will have a very prolonged life."

In other words: **"We worked hard to stop bulbs lasting longer, we must keep it up."**

It was only the Second World War that brought an end to the cartel.

Companies couldn't control international pricing and quality agreements while their countries were fighting each other.

But it does show you that making a better product can be bad for business.

Making an inferior product can actually be better business.

And, in case we feel superior, that's exactly the way advertising works.

Years ago, we used to make fun of the bad agencies for the poor quality of their work.

We said their motto was **"A good ad is a sold ad."**

That was all they cared about, whether the client bought it.

It would never occur to them to ask if consumers liked the ad, or if it worked.

"A good ad is a sold ad."

But now, that's pretty much all you hear in any agency: **"The client likes it."**

As if that's the sole job of advertising.

We don't care if it's an inferior product, just as long as the client buys it.

Just the same way light bulb quality was defined by its ability to make money.

We're not about making a better product, we're about making money.

THE CHURCH'S ROUND

The Anchor and Hope Baptist Church is a fundamentalist church in Canyon, Texas.

Their website reads: **"Two things every Christian should never leave home without: their gun and their Bible. One in the left hand, one in the right."**

They preach that one of man's biggest enemies is alcohol.

Also from their website: **"Habakuk 2:15 – Woe unto him that giveth his neighbour drink, that putest thy bottle to him and maketh him drunken also, that thou mayest look upon their nakedness."**

This church is convinced that 'craft' beers are simply alcohol's latest insidious disguise:

"Beer drinkers suffer from an inferiority complex because beer has none of the sophistication of wine, brandy and so forth while it is equally sinful. So the micro-brewery phenomenon started and the history, culture, and science of these brews has fascinated our country. Beer is somehow more respectable now."

But craft beer drinkers don't read their website, so the church took out a newspaper ad:

CRAFT BEER IS THE DEVIL'S CRAFT.

"Lot drank booze and committed incest – (Genesis 19:30)

Ben-Haddad drank booze and lost a war – (Kings 20:15)

The Israelites drank booze and lost their kingdom – (Isaiah 20:15)

Nabal drank booze and died in a coma – (Samuel 25:36)"

It concluded with an appeal to revoke the licences of the local bars and ban alcohol sales.

"Will we sell the youth of Canyon for the profits from booze?"

One local business saw this ad as an opportunity.

The Imperial Taproom is a large gastropub in Canyon, Texas.

They decided the church's ad could actually be used as a beer coupon.

They offered a dollar off the bill for every customer who brought in a copy of the ad.

They reproduced the ad on their Facebook page with the following copy:

"We are offering a dollar off your bill at Imperial Taproom in exchange for the 'Devil's Craft' coupon that was printed in The Canyon News on Sunday. We'll give you a dollar off for each one you bring in so feel free to bring multiple. Come and enjoy some devilishly good craft beers with us. We'll see y'all at the Taproom. Cheers."

The Taproom turned the church's campaign round 180 degrees.

Instead of being a campaign against craft beer it had become a coupon campaign FOR craft beer, advertising the Imperial Taproom.

It made the Taproom seem fun, the diametric opposite of the fire and brimstone church.

The church's ad will get seen and passed around, and a dollar or more off beer becomes a reason to visit the Taproom instead of your regular bar.

The Imperial Taproom's owners didn't have to spend a penny on advertising.

They let the church do their advertising for them.

All they had to do was call up the newspapers and TV and let them know about the offer.

Then they got all the free media coverage they could handle.

The Imperial Taproom demonstrated the martial arts way to respond to your competitor's advertising.

Don't oppose it, go with it, use its own force to defeat it.

Or, in our language, don't argue with core non-users of alcohol, they can't be converted.

Core non-users are the target for the church's advertising.

Ignore them and only talk to potential customers who are listening in.

Benefit by only targeting the people who can be influenced.

Or, as Napoleon said: **"Never interrupt your enemy when he is in the process of making a mistake."**

THE DOLLAR VALUE OF A LIFE

In Indiana, in 1978, three teenage girls were on their way to volleyball practice.

They stopped at a petrol station to fill up their Ford Pinto.

As they drove away, their petrol cap fell off so they stopped to retrieve it.

Before they could get out of the Pinto it was hit by a two-ton van travelling at 50 mph.

The petrol tank exploded and the three girls were burnt to death.

The van that hit them was found to contain empty beer bottles and marijuana.

So, the family of the three girls sued the van driver, right?

Wrong.

They sued Ford, the manufacturer of the Pinto.

Because the fault that caused the petrol tank to explode was known to Ford and could easily have been fixed, for just eleven dollars.

Ford admitted they knew about the fault, and in fact it had contributed to previous deaths, but they decided to do nothing about it.

So that's an open and shut case, right?

Wrong again.

Ford defended their decision to do nothing on the basis of risk/benefit analysis.

Under American law, if the cost of correcting a fault outweighed the cost of damage to the public, the manufacturer didn't have to correct it.

And so that was Ford's defence.

They produced the following numbers in court as their argument.

The cost of correcting the fault to the petrol tank was $11 per vehicle.

But the fault could be in eleven million cars and 1.5 million trucks, so the overall cost could be $137 million.

Whereas Ford calculated the number of deaths would probably be 180, the number of injuries also probably 180, and the numbers of destroyed vehicles 2,100.

Cost per death was estimated at $200,000, cost per injury $67,000, and cost per vehicle $700.

Which all added up to $49.5 million.

So, the benefit-versus-cost analysis worked out at $137 million to fix the fault versus $49.5 million to ignore it.

Obviously, it made financial sense to let a few people die.

The company was clearly behaving in a prudent, fiscally responsible fashion.

This argument was based on a precedent established by Judge Learned Hands in 1947.

The logic was that a company couldn't safeguard against every possible eventuality, so a reasonable compromise had to be struck.

The judge encapsulated this in his formula: $B < PL$.

Where B = cost of prevention, P = the probability of harm, and L = the cost of that harm.

Like most algorithms, it assumed that numbers were the only reality.

But of course, they aren't.

Ford was found not guilty based on this formula.

And if numbers were the only reality that would be the end of the matter, but it wasn't.

For us, the learning is that the trial irreparably damaged Ford's reputation.

Ford were seen as making dangerous, low-quality cars.

The management was seen as callous and uncaring about customers' lives.

Millions of Pintos had to be recalled to fix the problem, so no money was saved.

The chairman of Ford, Lee Iacocca, was fired.

And within a year the entire Pinto range was scrapped.

In a final piece of stupidity, six months after their deaths, the mother of the girls received a mass-mailing letter notifying her of the recall of her Ford Pinto.

To have the $11 safety modification fitted.

NONSENSE WRAPPED IN POSH LANGUAGE

Sabina and Ursula Eriksson were identical twin sisters from Sweden.

In 2008, they were on a coach from Liverpool to London.

The driver was suspicious of their behaviour and put them off at Keele services.

They were seen on CCTV walking along the central reservation of the M6.

Suddenly, they ran out into the speeding traffic, Sabina was hit by a SEAT.

Two police officers, Tracy Cope and Paul Findlayson, were called to the scene.

The BBC were filming a TV show *Motorway Cops*, so it was all caught on camera.

Surprisingly, as they arrived, the twins were calmly chatting.

But suddenly Ursula broke free and rushed back onto the motorway, straight under the wheels of a Mercedes truck going at 50 mph.

Then Sabina ran onto the motorway, straight into a VW Polo doing 70 mph.

On the soundtrack, you can hear the police officer's voice cracking as he radios: **"Ambulance to the scene, we've got two possible fatals."**

Other voices are saying: **"Jesus Christ, have you ever seen anything like that before?"** and **"No human body could survive that"** and **"She went up in the air like a rag doll."**

But they were more astounded when they found both sisters were still alive.

Ursula's legs had been crushed by the lorry.

But she started swearing, scratching, and spitting at the police.

Then Sabina started screaming and fighting, she punched Tracy Cope in the face and ran back onto the motorway.

It took five big men to get her and hold her down.

The police managed to handcuff her, both sisters were sedated and taken to hospital.

Ursula was kept in hospital, Sabina was arrested but allowed to leave.

In her confused state she was wandering the streets looking for her sister.

She met Glenn Hollinshead walking his dog, and stopped to stroke it.

They talked and, by chance, he was a trained paramedic. He asked if she'd like to use his spare room and next day he'd help her check the hospitals for her sister.

But the next day she stabbed him to death.

She left with a hammer, then walked along the street hitting herself in the head with it.

A motorist, Joshua Grattage, saw it and tried to stop her but she knocked him down with a roof-tile she had in her pocket.

Then she ran onto an overpass, forty feet above the A50 road, and threw herself off.

She broke both ankles and fractured her skull.

The police arrested her for murder.

Ursula and Sabina refused to comment, and tests showed no drugs in their systems.

The experts couldn't agree what was wrong with the twins.

They debated between **'Induced Delusional Disorder'** or **'Acute Polymorphic Psychotic Disorder'**.

But Glenn Hollinshead's brother had a different question: why was Sabina allowed out when she'd just tried to throw herself in front of motorway traffic THREE times?

When she'd been so crazy, screaming-swearing-spitting-punching, it had taken FIVE men to hold her down.

At least if she'd been held, his brother would still be alive.

The official answer was she'd been examined by three experts: 1) a police surgeon, 2) a psychiatrist, and 3) a social worker, who'd decided she was no danger to anyone.

So three experts couldn't spot what any normal person could spot.

That someone who repeatedly throws herself into traffic is disturbed and dangerous.

But experts with the right job title are entitled to opinions that outweigh common sense.

So we are forced to listen to experts, even when common sense tells us they are wrong.

Even when everything tells us it's just nonsense wrapped up in posh language.